MW00459785

THE
KARPMAN DRAMA
TRIANGLE
EXPLAINED

A Guide for Coaches, Managers, Trainers, Therapists
– and Everybody Else

by

CHRIS WEST

To Eric Berne and Stephen Karpman
Genius!

Copyright © 2020 by Chris West

The right of Chris West to be identified as the author of this work has been asserted
by him in accordance with the Copyright, Designs and Patents Act, 1988.

ISBN 978-0-9930233-6-1
Published by CWTK Publications
Cover Design by Blondesign

Contents

Moments

1

Chris and Emma need to sort a few things. He said he'd fix the bikes so they could go riding round the park, but the cycles are still in the hall with flat tyres and unrelaible brakes. The washing machine is making a funny noise. Should they just buy a new one? A couple of weeks ago Chris started sleeping in the spare bedroom when Emma got a nasty cold. She's better now but they're still sleeping apart.

Nothing big. A short, grown-up conversation should sort it all.

"We need to talk about a few things," Emma says on Saturday morning. She fixes a couple of coffees and opens a packet of those chocolate biscuits he likes. "Nothing heavy. Just little things." Emma says what these are.

"Anything else you'd like to put on my list?" he snaps. "God, you're so bloody controlling!"

"Controlling?" she begins, but he is already on his feet and stomping off towards the door, leaving her wondering what the hell she said. She feels it was all *her* fault, and an inner voice starts telling her that she *always* screws up like this. She feels that edge-of-tears sensation, just like she did when she was a kid.

They avoid each other for the rest of the day. The hurt subsides a bit, but won't go away. Next morning, Emma hears him get up early. She turns over and goes back to sleep.

Later Chris calls up that he's made breakfast. "I've done the bikes, too," he says.

Emma comes downstairs. There they are, ready to ride again. She knows she should say 'thank you', but instead, other words fly out of her mouth. "I don't want to ride those bloody things any longer." She regrets it instantly.

As she arrives at work on Monday, her boss smiles at her. She asks if Emma had a good weekend.

"Yeah, it was OK," Emma replies, grinning back. The actual content of the weekend is *not* something she wants to tell anyone about.

2

Jen is always getting into trouble. She drinks too much, and often pairs up with unkind men who treat her badly – the relationships never last long. Luckily her old school pal Sally is on hand to help out. If Jen rings up in the middle of the night to complain about the latest man, Sally will always listen. A couple of months ago, Sally bunked off work for an afternoon to spend some time with Jen after a particularly nasty break-up. Her boss wasn't impressed, and she's had to work extra late hours to get back in his 'good books'.

Sally's friends sometimes say she spends too much time and energy on Jen. "You've got to help your mates," she replies.

In more reflective moments, Sally feels envy of Jen – her own life, she feels, is a bit dull.

More recently, they went to a festival. When the time came to buy the tickets, Jen said she was really short of money that month. Could Sally lend her the cash? Sally agreed.

When they got there, Jen disappeared. Sally spent a nervous night in the tent: she'd not been to one of these events before. When Jen rolled in high as a kite at about five a.m., Sally complained. Jen said she was being boring and launched into a lecture on quite how boring she was.

Next morning, Jen apologized profusely, and they went and heard their favourite band. Sally enjoyed the music, and tells herself that she'd not have gone to the festival and heard it if it hadn't been for Jen.

Sally still hasn't got her money back.

3

A colleague confides in you, with a worried expression on her face, that her relationship is in deep trouble. She asks you for advice. You pause, then suggest she and her partner go off somewhere together for a break.

She shakes her head sadly. "We've done that. Can you suggest something more radical?"

"Have you tried seeing a counsellor?"

"Oh, yes, we tried that," she replies. "But it didn't work. She wasn't any good."

"Some of them aren't," you say sympathetically. "But I know someone who *is* good. A few years ago, when Sam and I were having a few difficulties, we went to see her, and she was great."

She frowns. "Counselling seems to work for some people, but I don't trust all this huggy, 'tell me all about it' stuff."

You think some more and come up with some more suggestions, but each one gets batted back with a reason why it won't work (or a reason why it might work for *you* but not for her).

Suddenly she turns on you. "I thought you knew about relationships, but you don't have a clue, do you?" she snaps and walks off in a huff.

You're left feeling puzzled and belittled. You did your very best to help. What did you say?

This feeling won't go away. At some point, you start feeling irritated with yourself, for not getting over this stupid, minor incident. You start criticizing yourself for being too sensitive. You lug this feeling of inadequacy round with you all day.

4

A young man enters the American High School where he is a student. He spots the girl who recently rejected his clumsy advances, now chatting with her mates by a side door. He walks towards her and calls her name. She turns, and a look of disdain fills her face.

A week ago, that look crushed him. Now he strides up to her. He launches into a tirade against her and against women in general.

"Those attitudes are mediaeval," she replies.

He reaches into his rucksack and gets out a gun.

She screams. The coach of the school football team hears this. He thinks of calling the cops, but a voice inside tells him he must take action and save the day himself. He begins to creep up behind the young man. He's nearly there, but the young man hears him and spins round.

"Hey, Rick..." the coach begins. He can't, perhaps, take the slightly patronizing tone out of his voice, as the gunman is such a loser on the sports field.

The young man pulls the trigger, and the big sports coach slumps to the ground. People are screaming now. A teacher comes out and tries to give first aid, but the young man tells her to 'back off'. She does so. Several other people are on their phones to the police, but nobody's arrived yet.

The girl, who has been rooted to the spot with fear, tries to remonstrate with the young man to hand the gun over, 'before anyone else gets hurt'.

"You made me do this," he says. He aims the gun at her – then turns it on himself and pulls the trigger again.

For years afterwards, those words echo in her head and she is stricken with guilt, mainly about the sports coach but also about the young man and those last words.

Chapter One

Introducing the Drama Triangle

Four apparently very different stories. A snapshot taken on the dismal road to relationship break-up. A relationship that will probably carry on – but maybe one day Sally will have had enough. A minor irritation (but one that seems to niggle more that it should. Why?) An event that ended two lives and blighted at least one other.

This book argues that they all have an unexpected amount in common. They can all be explained using the same psychological model. They could all have been avoided using that model. We can all learn from this model, and make our lives nicer, saner, kinder, easier and happier.

The model is the Drama Triangle. It was created by Dr Stephen Karpman MD, a California-based psychotherapist, in the late 1960s (his first paper on it came out in 1968). Since then it has been taken up by coaches, therapists, trainers and HR professionals around the world. However, I still meet many people who haven't heard of it. They 'get' the model almost at once when I start explaining it and soon want to know more. That's why I wrote this book.

Like all great models, Karpman's Drama Triangle is beautifully simple but capable of taking us to complicated places.

Here it is.

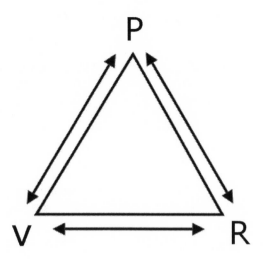

Just that.

The letters at each corner stand for three roles: **P**ersecutor, **V**ictim and **R**escuer.

Playing the *Persecutor* role means being a bully, a hater, an internet troll. It means controlling, threatening, criticizing, passing crude judgements, sermonizing, belittling, coming up with clever put-downs, solicitors' letters over trivial matters. It can mean acts of physical violence.

As a *Victim*, you find yourself – or think you find yourself – on the receiving end of such behaviour. You take it to heart. In some way, you get sustenance from it: it feels right. Note that if you are on the receiving end of Persecution but don't take it to heart, then you are not playing Victim. Eleanor Roosevelt said, 'No one can make you feel inferior without your consent'.

Playing the *Rescuer* role means charging in on a metaphorical white horse and sorting all this persecution and victimization out – but in a way that is more about looking or feeling good rather than doing good, a way that often leaves the people being 'rescued' as helpless as they were before.

The people in the stories above all played these roles, to differing degrees. They also lured other people into playing roles and they switched roles mid-story – which is the point of the *double-ended arrows* outside the triangle.

They were acting out Drama. They did so with great skill, born of plenty of rehearsal – but were totally unaware of the fact. Most would have thought that they were responding to circumstances in a way that, given the emotional logic of the situation, was perfectly reasonable. "That's how I am." "It's what I do." Others might have felt pain and wondered "Why do I get into situations like this so often?" or simply muttered "Here I go again…"

In fact, everyone in these stories has options to behave otherwise – but only if they understand why they're doing this stuff and do something about it. They are currently trapped in existing patterns, not just of behaviour, but of interpreting other people's actions, of beliefs and feelings about themselves and the world. These can be changed, if understood and challenged.

This Book is about Everybody
We probably recognized people we know in some of the above stories: 'difficult' people whose lives seem to be one lone Drama.

But this isn't just a book about 'other people'. We all do Drama. Yes, some do more than others, but the material in this book is universal. We can *all* make our lives better by understanding the Drama Triangle and changing our thinking and actions in the light of that.

A Dangerous Oversimplification

The Drama Triangle is sometimes oversimplified to present a world full of individuals neatly labelled 'Persecutors', 'Victims' or 'Rescuers'. The stories, however, show people playing various roles and moving from one role to another. Emma, for example, started out playing the Victim role, but switched to playing Persecutor.

Persecutor, Victim and Rescuer are roles that people play, not identities that people 'are'.

Most of us do have a 'favourite' role – we were probably taught it as children. Sally plays 'Rescuer' a lot. But it's still a stretch from spotting someone acting out a favourite role (again!) to sticking one of those three labels on them. Labelling is a form of Persecution.

It's a core tenet of this book that even the most eager Drama players are more than the roles they act out. We all have solid ground we can stand on to change this stuff.

The Dynamism of the Triangle

The arrows in the diagram, along the sides of the triangle, are very important. The real force of the model lies beyond the roles, annoying though they can be. It lies in what we *do* with the roles. Yes, we can simply act them out, but we can also play Games of lure and switch – which is where the real Drama kicks in.

There'll be a lot about Games, luring and switching in this book.

Stephen Karpman was a basketball player in his youth, and got the idea of the Triangle from his analysis of strategies in that sport – who stands where, who passes the ball to whom, who feints, who attacks, who defends. Think of a noisy, fast-moving basketball game rather than a static list of roles, and you'll get a better feel for the dark, busy energy of the Drama Triangle.

How this Book Works

I begin by examining each of the three roles in turn: Persecutor, Victim and Rescuer. I shall present some model role-players.

I shall then look at how they are *learnt*. Our parents (or whoever brings us up) encourage emotions that suit the roles and discourage emotions that don't. Our schoolmates, our close friends and our cultures do, too. As we grow up, we carefully watch and copy role-appropriate behaviours. We internalize beliefs and values that support our playing of the roles.

Aspects of our adult lives *encourage* us to keep on playing the roles, too.

I shall then look at how Drama 'works'. The *processes*. How it is set up and acted out. How people get lured 'onto the Triangle' and forced psychologically to act out roles they (probably) don't consciously want to. I shall look at 'switching', which is the most powerful tool in the Drama-player's armoury.

I shall look at environments that seem to encourage Drama.

After this, I shall take a more speculative look at the deepest reasons *why* we do this stuff. Chapter Ten is designed to 'sit behind' the earlier material, putting it in a full psychological context.

From Chapter Eleven onwards, I shall look at the practical steps we can take to *change* this. How do we stop doing this stuff? How do we shield ourselves and the people we care about from Drama and its consequences? How do we adapt our environments to lessen the likelihood of Dramas – our immediate environments, and the world itself?

My last chapter, Seventeen, will show how, having overcome Drama, we can *live without it*, as bigger and better people. In the end, the Drama Triangle does us a kind of favour. By showing us how not to live, it also shows us how to.

So let's start with those three roles: Persecutor, Victim and Rescuer...

Eric Berne and 'TA'

I mentioned 'Games' above, and you may be familiar with the book *Games People Play*, written by Eric Berne. My use of this term is deliberate.

Stephen Karpman, creator of the Drama Triangle, works within the tradition of Transactional Analysis (TA), the therapeutic approach created by Berne. Berne was a psychoanalyst (in other words, trained in the Freudian tradition), but broke away and created TA in the late 1950s / early 1960s. He disagreed with Freud's basic model (or at least adapted it radically). He also sought to demystify therapy, so that clients could work on themselves (guided by the therapist) rather than simply hand themselves over to a superior, all-knowing 'expert' to be 'cured'.

Berne was an amazingly original mind, with a superb eye for patterns of behaviour and a dark scepticism about protestations of good intent when things go wrong. Like Freud, he sought to create a big system that explained all (or much of) human dysfunction. I'm not sure he succeeded in this latter task – who has? However, he did create a tremendous toolbox for understanding ways in which people can mess up.

I use the TA toolbox a lot in this book, but this is not an uncritical guide to TA (I recommend one such book in the reading list at the end). I also use materials from other psychological and therapeutic approaches.

Chapter Two

The Persecutor Role

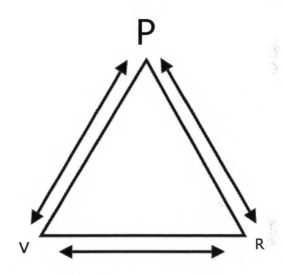

I'm not sure why I put the big letter P at the top. I guess I didn't want any trouble from any keen Persecutor players out there. Being at the top is where people want to be when they are acting the Persecutor role. They have to have the upper hand, to be 'top dog', to 'get one over' or be 'one up' on someone or some other people.

Karl is forever telling people (especially after a few drinks) how tough he is. He has a fund of stories of how he drove a competitor out of business or nailed a supplier to the floor (metaphorically, hopefully, though you never quite know with Karl). Taking another swill from his glass of overpriced wine (he buys the most expensive items on the menu, on principle), he says he has his wife where he wants her, too. And his mistress…

Chantal is beautiful. She dislikes ugly people. She thinks they are lazy. "If you make the effort to be beautiful, you can do so – or at least make the best of what you've got," she says, adding, "Even if that's not very much." People don't always like being told that, but Chantal reckons that they should be. If they ignore her advice, she reckons, they deserve whatever their ugliness brings them.

Jez spends a lot of time online. He often comes across content he finds 'offensive'. When he does, he tries to shame whoever posted it. The other day, he found a piece of cultural appropriation – an 18-year-old girl who had posted a picture of herself wearing a sari to a prom, even though she wasn't from India. "I really put that airhead in her place!" he says proudly. Oddly, it's often women he ends up shaming in this way.

Trevor spends a lot of time online, too. Using the anonymity of Twitter, he sends offensive messages to people who have annoyed him in some way. Recently, the central defender of the football team he supports scored an own goal. "I hope you die," Trevor messaged him. Politicians who diverge from his own views get this treatment, too.

B is in a gang. They rule the streets – well, a few streets of one of the poorer parts of town, anyway. They are not afraid to use violence to ensure this rule.

All these people spend a lot of time playing Persecutor.

Cindy is fiercely competitive. She is captain of her college hockey team and loves winning. Victory gives her a real buzz. But she doesn't look down on her opposition, and enjoys a drink with them after a match.

Is she playing Persecutor? No.

What makes the Persecutor role attractive?

We've been Trained for it – Emotionally

During childhood, some emotions are encouraged in us, while the expression (and thus, ultimately, the experiencing) of other emotions is discouraged.

When we expressed the *encouraged* emotions, we were rewarded by our parents (or 'significant others') with attention, love or at least a knowing nod. "That's my boy!" "Good girl!"

The person who plays Persecutor a lot was probably encouraged to express (and so feel) lots of anger, aggression and a sense of superiority.

They may have been taught fear, too. Learning to persecute is more about leaning to be tough rather than to be timorous. But lurking in many Persecutor mindsets is the sense that the world is a dangerous place, so you have to be the biggest bastard / meanest bitch in town to survive. Scratch a bully and you will often find, if not a coward, certainly someone who is carrying round a lot of fear. That had to come from somewhere.

By contrast, other emotions get *discouraged* in us as children. Our parents or significant others belittle or ignore us when we show these.

As training for the Persecutor role, sensitivity and empathy for others can be 'taught away' as weaknesses. "Show these, and you'll drop behind in the race of life / let the side down / not attract a mate."

Zak was a sensitive lad who loved art at school. But his dad dismissed such 'fancy stuff'. "Art is for sissies or oddballs. Go and play with the other boys in the park."

Veronica loved animals, but her mother thought they were dirty. "They carry all sorts of diseases. Did you know that you could get flu from cats?" She wouldn't allow Veronica the pet she craved. Loving animals, she said, was sentimental. "They're animals not people." ("Mind you," she would add at odd moments, "loving people isn't that brilliant either.")

It isn't just 'significant others' who do this training. Eric Berne believed that parents had the strongest influence; others have argued that peers do. Culture (in its broadest definition) can also be important. Maybe it's different for different individuals. What matters most is to understand that as we grow up there are powerful forces that programme us in Drama roles.

We've been Trained for it – Behaviourally

Zak, above, wasn't just encouraged to get angry; he was also shown how to do it. Dad would row with his mother in front of him. When he did this, he unconsciously gave his young son a masterclass in rage. Point your finger like this. Raise your voice – no, louder! Like this! Smash something – go on, that shows you're a real man doing this manly anger stuff properly!

Veronica's mother ran a Bitching 101 course especially for her. She would make snide comments about the friends she brought back from school. "Tricia is nice, but she does, well, smell a bit, doesn't she? I wonder if her parents are really *quite* the right sort."

Habitual postures (and other ways of self-presentation) can be modelled, too. Dad taught Zak a combative, swaggering, 'out-of-my-way' pose to use in general life. Veronica's mother had a kind of perpetual sneer. People playing Persecutor often talk loudly and with confidence, and use emphatic gestures (though remember that body language is also a cultural matter).

We've been Trained for it Intellectually: Interpretations, Beliefs and Values

We can learn to *interpret* what we experience in a role-appropriate way. The Persecutor player does a lot of this. Rather than just 'live and let live', in this role we can become judgemental, condemning other people's actions as 'weak' or 'disloyal'. (In Trevor's view, the central defender was both of these: he was inept and he 'let the team down', so deserved his death-threat tweet.)

We can acquire *beliefs* that support roles.

One belief that lies behind a lot of persecution is that life is what strategy theorists call a 'zero-sum game'. In such games, for every winner there has to be a loser. The struggle is a harsh one, too. No room for sentimentality in the world of the Persecutor (until they switch to another role, of course).

People who promote this view often refer back to Darwin and the evolutionary 'struggle for survival' which made us who we are and continues to underpin life.

This is very simplistic Darwinism, however. Our species evolved living in groups, not as solitary creatures (leopards, kingfishers, crocodiles and pandas have taken a different, 'loner' evolutionary route). Modern evolutionary thinkers also look at the survival value to group creatures like us of emotions that tie us to the group, such as sociability, helpfulness and concern for others. Philosophers add that we are more than just our evolutionary heritage, too. We have evolved moral systems and culture, without which we are not fully human.

Moral values ('shoulds') are a special kind of belief.

- 'Good people are x.'
- 'Bad people are y.'

Or, expressed in a more punitive way:

- 'I can only be a good person if I do x.'
- 'If ever I do y, I'm a bad person.'

Or, more punitive still:

- 'I can only be a good person if I feel / think x'
- 'If I even feel or think y, it shows I'm a bad person.'

Logically, values and factual beliefs are separate things, but in practice they intertwine in ways that are almost impossible to tease apart.

Beliefs and values are often summed up in, and implanted via, short, snappy maxims or slogans. Karl: "My dad always told me, 'Get your blow in first'."

As we grow, our minds begin to crystallize round a favoured role. We begin to discover supporting beliefs and values for ourselves and to incorporate these into our world-views. We begin to build a bank of <u>supporting evidence</u> for the beliefs and the values. Our (actually rather selective) <u>memory</u> can be particularly powerful. We recall times when the beliefs were justified (life is so varied that even the weirdest belief gets confirmed sometimes) and where the moral judgements felt appropriate.

The 'Schema'

All the forces described above are mutually supporting.

- Encouraged emotions
- discouraged (suppressed) emotions
- learned behaviours
- learned posture / gestures

- ways of interpreting what we experience
- beliefs about how the world is
- moral values
- maxims / slogans
- supporting evidence
- memories

All these work together to create what psychologists call a *schema* (pronounced 'skeemer'), a powerful, self-reinforcing mental framework though which we both interpret and react to the world.

Current Encouragements to Playing the Role

As if all this learning wasn't enough, there is plenty of encouragement around in our current environment to play Persecutor. Young men are bombarded with images of how they should be tough, in a brattish, aggressive manner. (Genuinely tough people are often pleasant and polite, except when the situation demands they turn on the toughness.)

Rudeness and aggression are modelled by certain politicians, by radio 'shock jocks', by some commentators on the internet. Politeness and compromise, which in reality make the world go round, are often belittled as weakness.

Current Payoffs to Playing the Role

Playing the role can also bring immediate benefits.

It can give us control. The Persecutor way of getting control is simply by grabbing it, by being angry, aggressive and bossy. Skilled Persecutors don't even grab power; they just assume it, acting as if they have it from the start. The rest of us often cede it.

Karl has done well in business by being a bully. I don't want to feed a stereotype here: many people do well in business by being original, approachable, reliable, thorough, hard-working, fair to their staff and loyal to their customers. But Karl has chosen a different route, and it has worked for him.

The 'sari' girl was very hurt by the criticism she received from a swarm of online Persecutors that Jez stirred up. She's never been quite her same bubbly self since – and that's his doing, a manifestation of his power.

The role can help our self-esteem. Playing the Persecutor role can make us feel good about ourselves. We feel big, tough, in charge.

The role can give us a 'get out' clause. All three Drama Triangle roles have 'get out' clauses that absolve players from the ordinary rules of politeness and respect for others.

For the Persecutor player, the get-out clause is that he/she is a superior being, above such rules. Karl likes to cite Nietzsche's distinction between 'master' and 'slave' moralities. "Some people take rules, other people make them," he says. Chantal thinks that rules are for ugly people. Jez sees himself in a different moral class to the people he shames. He thinks that their vulgarity or lack of political awareness needs to be criticized. If anyone suggests he actually has anger issues and can't control his temper, he says that his anger is 'righteous' and thus morally good. Our young gangster B sees life as a struggle. "Respect has to be earned," he says, gesturing to a scar on his face.

Our examples above, remember, aren't 'Persecutors', but people who play the Persecutor role a lot. They can be reasonable people at some times, and they can also play Victim or Rescuer, with great aplomb, when it suits them.

The Persecutor Role

Thuggish: Intimidate
or
Righteous: Criticize / Shame others

<u>The Schema</u>
Emotions Encouraged in Childhood
      Anger
      Aggression
      Superiority

Emotions Discouraged in Childhood (now Repressed)
      Weakness
      Sensitivity

Fear is Discouraged but Acquired Covertly

Learnt Behaviour
      Swagger
      Loud voice

Beliefs and Values
      Beliefs
            Life is a 'zero-sum game'
            Survival of the fittest
            The world is spoilt by bad people/attitudes
      Values
            (thuggish) Toughness/glamour
            (righteous) "My moral system (not anyone else's)"

<u>Current Encouragements to Playing the Role</u>
>Cult of 'toughness', especially in young men
>
>Rudeness in the media (especially online)

<u>Current Payoffs to Playing the Role</u>
Control
>Grabbed by the Persecutor…
>
>…or just assumed

Self-esteem
>Plenty – or a cover-up for too little?

Get-out Clauses
>"I'm superior…
>
>…The so-called rules of life don't apply to me."
>
>"My anger is righteous."

Chapter Three

The Victim Role

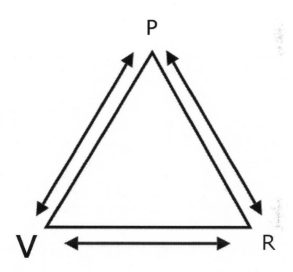

In the Victim role, we are – or believe we are – on the receiving end of the material in the above chapter. Things happen to Victims. They have no agency, no power.

"I'm trapped," says Maria. "I like my work, but hate my bosses. They're rude. They don't listen to me. But I can't leave. Think of the clients… And at my age, where will I get another job?" As a carer, she is actually very employable and could move relatively easily, but she has convinced herself that this is not the case.

For Mark, the entrapment is more about his relationship. He knows Fiona wants to get married, but he doesn't want to. Yet he's afraid to end things. On reflection, his life has always been like this. Stuck; in institutions (he went to a private boarding school), in 'friendships' with people he doesn't really trust.

Lewis has got into debt, another form of trappedness.

Nik is trapped in a longing for 'the old days', when he played in a grunge band and was a rebel. He ended up having to get a 'proper job', which he hates.

Persecutor players can also play Victim when it suits them. Get Karl onto the subject of how hard-working businessmen are treated by government and unelected bureaucrats…

Victim narratives always blame someone else. Maria blames her bosses. Mark blames his parents for being rich and sending him away to school. Lewis blames his family for being poor and making him feel that to be big in the world you had to splash money about. Nik still blames everything on Margaret Thatcher.

Suggest to people playing Victim that they actually get up and do something about their predicament, and you're likely to end up being told, "It's all right for you…" or "You don't know what it's like for me."

In Victim mode, people often make mountains out of molehills. They 'sweat the small stuff'. Mark is still furious about some comment Fiona made six months ago. Nik has a long-running row with the council about where his bins get put after they've been emptied. This obsessing about petty things all goes to stoke and reward that Victim sense of being trapped – hemmed in by all these mountainous molehills towering up around them.

In Victim mode, people also keep adding to the molehills by being difficult and alienating people. Nik's expletive-filled letter to the Head of the Sanitation Department did not help his cause.

False modesty is playing Victim. "Oh, I'm not very good at singing really." This invites a Rescue: "Oh, go on, you're brilliant."

Genuine modesty is not playing Victim, of course. It is authentic and not 'playing' anything. In practice, however, one can shade into the other – a naturally modest person might suddenly find themselves 'overdoing it a bit' in a stressful situation. Entering the Triangle isn't always a great leap or startling gesture. One can wander on to it unawares.

What makes the Victim role attractive? Here are some points about the Victim schema.

Encouraged Emotions
Passivity and *helplessness* are common ones. Maria was taught to 'Be a good girl' and be quiet. Mark was institutionalized from the age of 8, where he was taught to follow the crowd and the rules.

Sadness is another encouraged emotion. It can be praised as a sign of sensitivity. I'm not arguing that sadness is always a Victim emotion. It's a natural part of life. But when people overplay it or equate it with virtue, it stops being natural and becomes part of a role, an act.

Self-pity is another key Victim emotion. Victim players learn to really enjoy victimhood.

I talked about *fear* and Persecutors, but it is also often part of the

Victim sensibility. It is rarely consciously taught to either type: few parents tell their kids, "Go on, be afraid! No, *really* afraid – like this!" But they can model fear for the observant, eager-to-learn child.

Discouraged Emotions

Emotional training for the Victim role can involve the discouragement of *energy* and of *self-expression*. *Exuberance* and high spirits are looked down on as somehow vulgar or unworthy.

Maria was told, "Nice children don't do that!" Mark was allowed to be a bit boisterous – after all, his parents said, he is a boy – but never to say anything that might offend anyone.

In the extreme, Victim training can discourage any display of emotion at all. At this level, the child internalizes a terrible fear that if they let feelings out, their world will fall apart. This is crippling, but provides an illusory sense of importance. (Usually, the reality is that if he or she lets feelings out, there'll be a slight disturbance then life will go on.)

Behaviours

As with the Persecutor role, various Victim behaviours will have been learnt. Maria's mum loved a good moan, and has passed this skill – vocabulary, tone of voice, subject matter – on to her daughter.

There are Victim postures and gestures to learn. These can include walking with a slight stoop, avoidance of eye contact and a limited sense of one's own space. Persecutor players often act as if they have a large balloon of space around them, like a nation that suddenly claims extra territorial waters; Victim players can do the opposite. The subconscious giving off of 'vibes' that come with these poses can be powerful signals.

In Victim, we often speak quietly, sometimes with a whining tone –

though some people, especially those who more usually play Persecutor, play this role loud and clear, to ensure that the world hears their moaning.

Interpretations, Beliefs and Values that Support the Role

Part of 'Victim training' is learning to interpret actions and events as threats. A harmless gesture or word can be read by a keen Victim player as aggression. Paranoia is an extreme version of this.

People who interpret things in this way often switch quickly to Persecutor. The drunk in the pub who wheels on you with "Who are you looking at?" is coming on as Persecutor, but their first reaction was to interpret your brief, innocent glance as something Persecutory by you, which made them into a Victim.

The Victim *belief* system may mirror that of the Persecutor one, that life is a zero-sum game. The difference is that the Victim version accepts losing out in that harsh game rather than Persecuting in order to make sure they win it.

In Victim, we may believe that the odds in the game are stacked against 'people like us' from the start. "We're going to lose anyway, so why fight?"

Victim *values* can highlight the virtue and nobility of suffering.

Maria goes to mass every Sunday, looks up at the crucified figure over the altar and reminds herself that even the Son of God suffered a terrible death.

Mark has no time for religion, but believes that serious culture shows us that suffering makes us deep, worthwhile people. Happy people, he thinks, are frivolous and shallow.

Nik takes this further: happy people are actively bad. Anyone who succeeds, he says, does so by lying, cheating or stealing. Look at the Karls of this world…

Current Encouragements to Playing the Role
The contemporary world is full of encouragement for us to play Victim. There are two main sources.

Many commentators on modern society say we are a *Victim Culture*. In such a culture, if you can lay claim to Victimhood, you immediately become beyond criticism. If you're not a Victim in some way, you are regarded as 'part of the problem' and not worth listening to.

A second source is certain strains of *politics*. 'Strong-man' politicians and their supporters use fear as a tactic to get people to support them. Bombard people with 'fake news' or opinion pieces about how decent folk are under threat from evil and powerful outsiders of various kinds (Muslims, Jews, financial elites are three examples used a lot), and they will turn to a strong-sounding leader for protection. In other words, make people feel they are Victims, and they will seek Rescue.

There's a debate about how pervasive this bombardment is. Some people deny it, and say the media always prefer bad news because it attracts attention: new media, same old story. Others think there is a full-blown conspiracy out there. Either way, much of modern media encourage Drama.

Current Payoffs to Playing the Role
Playing Victim can have payoffs, too. Despite the Victim's apparent helplessness, playing the role can actually bring plenty of *control*, especially through manipulating others' guilt. Victim players who do this will still insist they are unfortunate Victims, even when guilt-stricken people are running round them doing their bidding.

Victim players can also attract Rescuer players to help them (or to appear to help them, anyway: more on this below): another form of control.

If you believe that only Victims are truly virtuous, the role can provide a kind of inverted *self-esteem*, the self-esteem of the martyr. Beneath that, Victim players tend to lack real self-esteem.

They can, at least be open about that lack. After a few drinks, Mark will often admit to hating himself. This is potentially an opportunity for growth via tackling such irrational self-dislike. But Mark also thinks that all therapists are sandal-wearing tossers – he can slip neatly into Persecutor when he has to – so don't expect much progress there in the near future.

The Victim *get-out clause* from the rules of life is the terrible (as they see it) nature of their suffering. They are below the law. The rules were made by the successful / lucky / beautiful / rich / ruthless / privileged / clever, and so the Victim isn't obliged to keep to them.

The Victim role is a boundless source of excuses

Life can deal lousy hands to some people. Shouldn't we have sympathy? Of course. But playing Victim is no way out of a bad place – instead, it just keeps people there.

The Victim Role

No power
No agency, no responsibility
Trapped…
    And it's *all* somebody or something else's fault!

The Schema
Emotions Encouraged in Childhood
    Helplessness
    Sadness
    Self-pity
    Fear

Emotions Discouraged in Childhood (now Repressed)
    Boisterousness
    The pleasure of self-expression
    (Worst case) Any emotion at all

Learnt Behaviour
    Humble posture
    Limited sense of personal space

Interpretations, Beliefs and Values
    Interpretations
        Sees threats and slights where these aren't intended
    Beliefs
        ? Zero-sum game
        Personal unworthiness
    Values
        Suffering = Virtue

Current Encouragements to Playing the Role
Victim culture

Strongman politicians seeking to frighten people

Current Payoffs to Playing the Role
Control

Through manipulation of other's guilt

Attracting Rescuers (see next chapter)

Get-out clause

'Beneath the law'

"The rules were made by the successful/lucky/rich (etc.)...

....They don't apply to me."

Free from ultimate responsibility

A boundless source of excuses

Chapter Four

The Rescuer Role

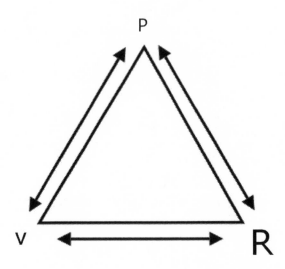

Rescuer players, unsurprisingly, come to the rescue. This sounds admirable. But...

They can rush in before they are asked. Of course, sometimes the 'rescuee' can't ask: an unconscious person lying by a busy highway, for example. But usually this isn't the case. The rescuee is perfectly able to ask but doesn't get a chance to. The knight on his or her white horse just charges in.

Sheila is busy at her computer. Something isn't working with the formatting, but she's beginning to get the hang of it. Then Brian appears. "Let me help!" he says. Before Sheila can object, he is leaning over her and clicking away at her keyboard.

Having charged in, the Rescuer may find that they haven't the resources or skills to do anything effective. Brian doesn't sort Sheila's problems, and actually manages to delete a section of text she has been working on. (He then becomes overly apologetic and starts bemoaning how he 'always screws up' – a 'Switch', of which much more later.)

Rescuers can also respond to calls for help, charge in and suddenly find they don't have what it takes (time, resources, commitment) to actually solve the problem. If too much of these resources are asked of them, the Rescuer can start resenting it – another 'switch' to Victim.

Even if they don't achieve much, Rescuer players make a big fuss of the rescue. The person being rescued is expected to be grateful, even if the rescue doesn't really work. Rescuer players enjoy the mission more than the result.

In the long run, rescuing can create and sustain *dependency*. Truly helping people puts them back on their feet. Compulsive Rescuers often find subtle ways of making sure the rescuee never quite gets there, and remains reliant.

While they are on their grand missions, Rescuer players can ignore the needs of the people close to them. Dickens' Mrs Jellyby was too busy with a charitable project in Africa (which didn't actually work) to look after her family.

In Rescuer mode, we can find it incredibly hard to accept favours from other people. We always feel the need to reciprocate, while the other person is often simply doing what they think is right and doesn't require any such reciprocation, just a friendly and sincere 'thank you'.

Rescuer players can be know-alls, always ready with an answer to rescue other people from their ignorance.

Maria, whom I introduced in the previous chapter, is in a rescuing profession. But most of the time she is not Rescuing (I'm going to use a capital R for the role playing), just helping people who need help, who have requested it and whom she has the resources and skill to help. She can drift into Rescuing, however. Bert could actually get up and dress himself, but he plays the Victim and Maria rushes in to help. Ettie often has little emergencies that Maria has to sort out. When Maria was off work for a month, Ettie's emergencies stopped.

There is another form of Rescuing, which can be more passive. It is setting oneself up as a 'goody-goody', signalling virtue like crazy. "Look what a good person I am!"

This annoys the hell out of other people, setting up a switch whereby they (the others) get angry with the goody-goody (= start playing Persecutor) and switch them (the virtue signaller) to Victim.

Readers might object that you have to stand up for what you believe in. Of course. But we all know the difference between someone who states their values when asked or when they feel it is necessary, and the individual who lets you know in the first five minutes that they have the complete set of currently fashionable views on all social issues.

Jez, the online Persecutor of the politically incorrect that we met in Chapter Two, can play Rescuer brilliantly in this 'virtue signalling' way.

Let's look at the Rescuer schema.

Encouraged Emotions
Many of the emotions encouraged in training for Rescuer role are

admirable: the *confidence* to 'leap in', the *pleasure of helping others,* best of all, *compassion.* The key in stopping Rescuing is to keep these but ditch the Drama.

Rescuer players are often very *sociable.* Persecution can be alienating from others, as can be the experience of playing Victim, but Rescuing needs people to rescue. People who Rescue a lot can take this further and radiate *perpetual cheeriness.* This becomes wearisome to others after a while (and must be exhausting to keep up). It can be crucifying to the Rescuer player if a loss needs mourning.

(Not every Rescuer player is sociable. Older readers may remember the TV hero *The Lone Ranger,* who rode into town, righted a wrong, then rode off again into the sunset, alone apart from his faithful but taciturn Native American sidekick, Tonto.)

Another Rescuer emotion is *disappointment,* when the world isn't grateful enough for your amazing efforts at rescuing.

Discouraged Emotions
Rescuer training, like Persecutor training, discourages any show of weakness. Rescuers have to be strong.

Rescuers are taught to feel bad about meeting their own needs. In many cultures, this is a message given particularly to women – but there are male Rescuers out there, too.

Sadness can be discouraged. "Come on, cheer up! It's not as bad as all that!" Sometimes these words are necessary and helpful. At other times they can halt the natural process of mourning a loss.

Behaviours
When acting this role, people often have a busy, focused posture.

Rescuers can be in a hurry, like emergency ambulances. *Nee-nah! Nee-nah! I'm on my way to a Rescue!* Quite right for the ambulance, of course, but less so for the perennial Rescuer player.

The Rescuer voice tone can be shrill.

Interpretations, Beliefs and Values

Rescuer beliefs and values are often healthier than that of Persecutors or Victims. Rescuers don't see the world as a struggle of all against all. They understand that we can and should help one another. The problem with Rescuing is how that helping is done. Potentially good stuff is done in the wrong way at the wrong time with the wrong emotional baggage.

Less positively, Rescuer training can involve learning to interpret complex events as simple good guy / bad guy interactions.

Rescuer beliefs tend not to put much faith in people's abilities to stand up for themselves. Rescuers can discount human 'oomph', feistiness and ability to fight back – they need Victims to Rescue.

Current encouragements to Playing the Role

There are plenty of Rescuer role models out there, and many of them, unlike the Persecutor and Victim ones, are good. Rescuing as a Triangle role is about following these models in an unhelpful way.

Current payoffs to Playing the Role

Rescuer players can get *power* from making other people dependent.

Rescuing is very good for the *self-esteem*. "When I'm up there on my white horse, putting the world to rights, I am a good person." However, this can morph into "I am *only* a good person when I am up there putting the world to rights."

The Rescuer *get-out clause* is the virtue of their mission. Rescuer players think that, like emergency ambulances, they are allowed to crash through life's red lights and drive on the wrong side of the road, while the rest of us are supposed to get out of the way and do so with a look of admiration.

The Rescuer Role

Pile in…
>   Without being asked
>   When rescue is not really needed
>   Without the right resources
>   Expecting gratitude
>   Enjoying the buzz
>   Creating dependency

'Passive' Rescuing
>   Excessive virtue signalling

The Schema
Emotions Encouraged in Childhood
>   Enjoyment of helping
>   Sociability
>   Relentless cheerfulness
>   Disappointment

Emotions Discouraged in Childhood (now Repressed)
>   One's own needs

Behaviour
>   In a hurry
>   Shrill tone

Interpretation
>   Sees any conflict as something they have to solve
>   Oversimplification: good guys vs. bad guys

Beliefs/Values

> Are admirable when done right...
>
> ...but not when overbearing
>
> Human strength often discounted

Current Encouragements to Playing the Role

> Plenty of good rescuing about...
>
> ...but Rescuer players do it all wrong

Current Payoffs to Playing the Role

Control

> Making others dependent

Self-esteem

> Being one of the good guys

Get-out Clause

> "I'm on a mission! Get out of my way!"
>
> *"Nee-nah, nee-nah!"*

Note: it isn't all bad news

I've painted a pretty dark picture of the three roles above, but the roles aren't all bad – which is another part of the reason why everybody plays them.

Rescuing is the obvious example of a role sometimes being useful and good. Helping is great – when we are best placed to do so and when we do so with a minimum of fuss and a genuine desire to see the rescuee back on their feet and flourishing.

Sometimes we do need to, if not actively *Persecute*, get very angry and/or bossy. It is better to shout at people to get the hell out of a burning building rather than waiting politely for them to finish what they are doing then quietly suggesting they might like to go elsewhere.

Anger, which can be a powerful Persecutor emotion, evolved to give us extra energy to fight back when things got tough. When our ancestors were faced by a hungry sabre-toothed tiger, they got angry and survived.

Maybe we never need to be *Victims*, but we all have to deal with defeat and loss. Sadness, a Victim emotion, is part of that process. Pretending a major loss hasn't happened is not an option. Such pretence just stores up pain, which will get released in a dysfunctional way later. Knowing what it's like to lose and suffer makes us better, bigger people, too. The Victim belief that suffering engenders virtue has a measure of truth to it.

We put ourselves on the Drama Triangle at those times when we take up one of the three roles in a way that *doesn't* suit the realities of the situation, where the personal emotional reward of playing the role is more important than any objective, practical effect it will have, where we are acting out damaged 'old stuff' rather than responding appropriately to what's happening now.

Stephen Karpman argues that even in these cases, there is a small percentage of the motivation that is authentic and appropriate – it just gets distorted and magnified by the old stuff.

Sally in Story Two, for example, gets something out of her relationship with Jen. She probably wouldn't have gone to the festival without her friend, and she did enjoy listening to the band – even if she's unlikely ever to see that ticket money.

Questionnaire

Here are some questionnaires to fill in, to help you look at how and why you play the three roles.

In answering them, be honest. We all do this, so there's no shame in admitting to it. And nobody else need see your answers!

Fill one set in quickly – don't spend too long over answering them. Live with your answers for a bit, then revisit what you said. Fill in a new page if you feel you need to do so, but keep the old one. In a second filling-in of the form, you might find yourself censoring your initial answers, but later still you may realize these were truthful and want to come back to them.

If you really can't think of an answer (for example, to the question about parental 'maxims'), then leave it blank for the moment. Keep pondering it. Maybe something will suddenly come to mind.

When was the last time I played the Persecutor role?

What happened?

How did I feel?

When I was a child, did my parents (or other significant people I copied) act out this role?

What did they do?

Did they have a maxim or slogan that supported this behaviour? (If so, what was it?)

When was the last time I played the Victim role?

What happened?

How did I feel?

When I was a child, did my parents (or other significant people I copied) act out this role?

What did they do?

Did they have a maxim or slogan that supported this behaviour?
(If so, what was it?)

When was the last time I played the Rescuer role?

What happened?

How did I feel?

When I was a child, did my parents (or other significant people I copied) act out this role?

What did they do?

Did they have a maxim or slogan that supported this behaviour? (If so, what was it?)

Most of us have a 'favourite' role, which we probably got most training at as children and which we now play more than others...

Which role do I play most often?

Reading the descriptions of the three roles, did I find myself more sympathetic to one? If so, which one?

How did that feel? Exciting? Embarrassing? Where do you feel this?

Did my parents (or other significant others in my childhood) act out one role more than another? If so, which one?

How does it feel to remember this?

The 'feeling' questions are to check the power of your reactions. If the feelings were strong, you have probably rediscovered some early role training. You can now use this awareness: if you feel a situation you are in is making you feel these same reactions, old stuff is being restimulated. Once you have read this book, you will be able to note this and choose to respond to the situation in new, more helpful ways.

Chapter Five

Where it all Takes Place: The Subconscious

Almost all the acting out of the roles is done at a subconscious level. This might seem an obvious point, but it's important to be crystal clear about this, otherwise some of the material in this book will seem contrary or downright weird.

The human mind is often compared to an iceberg, those floating islands of ice of which around only 10% is visible to the mariner. The 10% is the conscious mind, and the remaining 90% is the subconscious.

This image doesn't do justice to the vastness of the subconscious. It has been estimated that not 90% but 98% of our brainwork goes on there. The percentage of which we are conscious is tiny.

The subconscious does all sorts of good things for us. You drive through a busy city, navigating, watching out for other road-users of all kinds, checking your speed and all the other tasks associated with urban driving. As you do this, you listen to music and ponder a meeting coming up next week. And all the time, your brain is monitoring your physical state, your breathing, your posture, whether the environment out there is safe, your need for food and water... Our subconscious is amazing!

But it is also flawed. Forget the iceberg image and think of a badly built IT system. Parts of the subconscious do not communicate with other parts. Parts can even fight with other parts – this was Sigmund Freud's basic insight: mental illness is war between mutually uncomprehending parts of the subconscious. The subconscious is not good at making itself clear to, or at listening to, the conscious mind, either. In evolutionary terms, it hasn't had much practice. Exactly when and how humanity developed the self-monitoring skill called 'consciousness' is a mystery. The philosopher Julian Jaynes reckons that our ancestors acquired it as recently as 3,000 years ago.

Even if Jaynes is wrong and we've had consciousness for a lot longer, it is still new by evolutionary standards. Our ancestors began to develop bigger brains three million years ago. These tripled in size over this time (till about 200,000 years ago, since when the growth has stopped). As evolution has been going on for 3.8 billion years, this is incredibly fast growth. It is not surprising that this new product still has plenty of 'bugs'. Our brain, with its conscious mind, is still at the Beta-testing phase. Who's doing the testing? We are.

The result of all the above is that we can be motivated by forces, often conflicting ones, of which we have no clear understanding. Our conscious mind can end up as a puzzled observer of our own behaviour. Hence the "Why the hell did I do that?" feeling that follows a Game or (sometimes) Triangle role-playing. The unconscious can also spend its time providing justifications for behaviour. "Ah! I must have done it for reason X." The answers it comes up with may well be false: actually, the reasons were Y and Z, but the subconscious doesn't want to say that, because another part of it would disapprove.

For example…

Chris from Story One once lost some tickets to the opera that Emma had been given by an aunt. He had soccer practice planned for that evening, but Emma had insisted he come with her.

When she accused him of deliberately losing them, he got angry: "Are you saying that I've hidden them under the doormat and am now lying to you?"

"No, but you meant to lose them, in some way."

"What do you mean? How did I 'mean to lose' them? That's ridiculous!"

Emma didn't know how to reply – but two days later, she accidentally dropped a vase given to them by Chris' uncle. He instantly rounded on her and said, "You did that on purpose, didn't you?"

The subconscious has its own get-out clause: "I didn't mean it." Chris was annoyed at being accused of deliberately losing the tickets, because the allegation was literally untrue. He didn't consciously intend to lose them. However, his subconscious organized things so that the tickets got lost (he found them a few days after the performance, in the pocket of a coat he doesn't usually wear; he didn't tell Emma). Emma didn't mean to drop the vase, but it still ended up in pieces on the floor.

Self-sabotage is a common manifestation of the subconscious at work in an unhelpful way.

A family friend dropped out of university, where he had studied hard, a month before his finals.

In 2001, British businessman Gerald Ratner destroyed his family jewellery company by saying, in a speech at London's Institute of Directors, that he could sell one of his products cheaply because it was 'total crap', adding that another product cost less than a prawn sandwich from a major foodstore and probably wouldn't last as long.

Eric Berne talked of 'gallows humour'; comic things people say while they are in a subconsciously driven self-destruction process. "Look at me. I must be mad to do this. But, hey, here I go again!"

The rise of social media has given people great opportunities for subconscious self-sabotage. A thought comes to your mind; you type it into Twitter; you press 'Tweet'. Five minutes later you think, 'Oh, my God, did I just say that?' Yes, you did, and it's there for everyone to see, forever (or for the foreseeable future, anyway). Facebook gives us the chance to write longer pieces that make us look even more stupid or unpleasant.

Self-sabotage can include just having a quick beer or three before giving a speech, or setting off late for an important appointment. Freud was particularly keen on tactless slips of the tongue.

Freud, of course, had a particularly dark view of the subconscious (or *un*conscious as he called it). He saw it as a place where three tyrants resided, each trying to control the psyche for its own ends, ruthlessly, deviously and unrelentingly.

Most modern psychologists don't see things quite as fatalistically as that. We can work with our subconscious, which in the end wants to help us, even if it can be utterly inept at times. We can teach it to respond in ways we wish (even if it isn't always a perfect pupil). We can learn to listen to it. We can adapt our conscious selves (where acceptable) to its desires. 'Know thyself,' taught the ancient Greek philosopher Socrates. The second half of this book, from Chapter Eleven onwards, will show some ways of working towards these goals.

The Subconscious

Even more <u>hidden</u> than an iceberg
>98% of our brainwork goes on there

<u>Amazing!</u>

But…

<u>Divided</u>
>One part can be at war with another
>And we have no conscious awareness of the fact

<u>Parts can be:</u>
>Powerful
>Shrewd
>Devious

<u>Does not communicate well with conscious awareness</u>
>Does not directly say what it wants
>Does not listen

<u>Makes us do things that we don't 'mean' to do</u>
>The missing opera tickets and the broken jug

<u>But we can learn to deal with it</u>
>'Re-programming' it a bit
>Listening to it better
>Accepting it and adapting our self-image

Chapter Six

Acting out the Roles 1:
The Invitation and the Buy-in

Back to one specific aspect of the subconscious at work: Drama.

At its simplest, we can simply act out Drama Triangle roles in our imaginations. This is *inner drama*. Sometimes dramas just pop into our heads. Other times we sit back and tell ourselves a story.

For some people, this can be disturbing. Kezia's inner dramas don't always go in directions she likes. She recently went to a therapist, who reassured her that many people have this experience. The therapist said that Kezia could even be proud of the fact that she is sensitive and imaginative. Having a wild and sometimes unkind imagination doesn't mean we are damaged or dangerous. What matters is how we actually *act*.

Kezia will be able to use this book to distance herself from these inner dramas and understand them better.

However, the focus of this book is on how the roles get played *in public*.

Getting Someone Else onto the Triangle

In its most basic public form, someone can just start playing a role, just as a busker can stand on a street corner, take out a ukulele and start strumming it. But the Drama only really begins when a second person *responds* – for the ukulele strummer when a Rescuer player throws them some money, a Victim player complains how the noise is hurting their ears, or a Persecutor player tells them to shut the f*** up.

Drama doesn't just 'begin', of course. It is *set up*. (Remember, this is rarely done consciously.) Someone has offered what Eric Berne called a 'Game Invitation' by acting out a role, and someone else has responded.

Game Invitations can be general or targeted. A *general* Invitation is where the Invitation-issuer just starts playing a role and sees if anyone responds. ("Anyone want to do some Drama today?") This is what happens in the ukulele example above. A *targeted* Invitation is issued to an individual: the Invitation-issuer spots a likely responder and then offers the Invitation by starting to play a Triangle role. ("Hey, you. Yes, you! Let's do some Drama!")

Either way, Drama begins when a Game Invitation is issued and hits a nerve in another person, who responds.

Some terminology. I call this nerve the responder's *hot button*. Hitting the nerve is *pressing* this button. When the responder takes this bait and starts to play one of the roles, too, I call this *buying in* to the Drama. The responder has been *hooked* by the original Invitation-issuer (the *initiator*), who has made them a *sucker*.

That last term, 'sucker', may sound harsh. But that's what has happened. The initiator has essentially invaded the sucker's space, hacked into their head and has started to manipulate them.

The Drama begins

- The *initiator* issues a *Game Invitation.*
- The Invitation *presses* the sucker's *hot button*
- The sucker accepts, *buying in* by starting to play a Drama Triangle role, too. They've been *hooked.*

Pastimes

Early attempts at setting up Drama often involve the initiator getting the sucker (or suckers, in the plural) onto the <u>same</u> Triangle corner, to carry out what Eric Berne called *pastimes*. (Berne also turned that into a verb: participating in such an interaction was 'pastiming'.)

Here are some pastimes being pursued in on a Saturday afternoon in a British pub, The Duke's Head...

A group of young male United supporters have gathered in the public bar. It's the local derby tonight, and the boys are getting drunk in anticipation of it. "We'll p*ss all over them!" shouts a burly man who looks like the leader of the gang. "And their supporters!" shouts another.

In the smarter, 'saloon' bar, two retired gentlemen, Bill and George, listen to the row and bemoan the state of the world. "People didn't behave like that in the old days," says Bill. George nods. "Well, what do you expect?" he says. "Look at the politicians we have nowadays – they're all crooks." (Berne called Bill and George's pastime, moaning about the current world, 'Ain't it awful'. It is the staple fare of much comment, not just in pubs but traditional print media (especially 'redtop' newspapers) and even more in modern social media, with its plethora of opinionated 'bubbles'.)

Tammy and Fran are in a different corner of the saloon. Students at the local college, they aren't moaning about the world: they are planning to save it. People will stop using plastic. Everyone will turn vegan. A global government, committed to Socialism, will emerge. So far, they haven't actually done anything to bring these ends about, but one day...

In all three cases, a group of people is jointly acting out one of the roles. There is no confrontation, so it's a kind of semi-Drama, like a story that doesn't go anywhere. The United supporters, all playing Persecutor, will most likely turn up at the game, shout some insults at the visiting fans (who are safely cut off from them by a fence and a line of stewards), then head back to the pub; nobody will get hurt. Bill and George will enjoy their Victim moan, then go back to their actually very comfortable homes in streets that are safer than most streets in the town, let alone on the planet. Tammy and Fran may well become genuine activists – but today they'll just sit and talk Rescuer talk.

Even these scenarios were set up, however.

The burly man is the leader of the gang. He and some of his mates set the agenda and the tone. The followers are the suckers, who just join in.

Bill and George often meet, and conversation often goes down the same road. But they don't consciously meet to moan, just to 'catch up'. At some point one of them sets the conversation in that direction (the initiator) and the other one follows (the sucker).

Tammy and Fran have a similar dynamic. They didn't agree to meet up and save the planet, but once one of them turned the conversation in that direction, the other followed.

In all these cases, someone has got someone else (or, with the burly man and the fans, some other people) to join them playing a Triangle role.

The payoffs to pastimes are obvious. They enable us to act out familiar (and, in the past, rewarded) roles. They bring people together.

Sadly, people can get bored with this, however…

Role Competition

If another group of United fans came into the pub, they might seek to outdo the first lot in bluster and aggressive talk.

George and Bill might decide to have a Victim competition, swapping ever-greater despair at modernity. The classic Monty Python *Four Yorkshiremen* sketch is a parody of this, with each participant trying to outdo the youthful miseries endured by the other 3.

Tammy and Fran can find themselves competing to be the most virtuous.

Some writers believe that much Drama is actually role competition. In their ebook, *How to Break Free of the Drama Triangle and Victim Consciousness*, Barry and Janae Weinhold go even further and argue that Drama is caused by people competing for one role, that of Victim. This is an interesting idea, but I think that is just one type of Drama. There are other motivations and types.

Conflict and Complement

Full-on Drama really kicks in when someone on one corner of the

Triangle tries to initiate a situation where the sucker is offered a *different* role. A Persecutor player hooks a Victim. A Victim player hooks a Persecutor. A Victim player hooks a Rescuer. A Rescuer player hooks a Victim (and, ideally, a Persecutor, too). And so on.

That is what happened in the four stories at the beginning of this book. The initiators weren't just looking for a fellow Persecutor, Victim or Rescuer player to pastime with or even outdo – they were looking for a *complement* to *conflict* with. In Story One, Chris' angry outburst turned Emma into a Victim. Sally needs a Victim to rescue in Story Two. Story Three – I'll look at that later. Story Four started when the boy called out his ex's name, probably in quite a forceful manner: Persecutor. She fought back: a brief competition to be the biggest Persecutor followed. When the gun appeared, she lost that contest and became what he wanted her to be, the Victim. This was a targeted Game Invitation on his part. But there was also a general Game Invitation, open to anyone present, which hooked the unfortunate sports coach.

So, now we have an initiator and a sucker or several suckers, on the Triangle and acting out complementary roles. What happens next?

They may simply remain in their roles, like two tennis players getting ready for a game by lobbing a ball back and forth.

They may *escalate* the intensity of the role-playing (more on this later). Chris could have shouted louder at a now tearful Emma, or they could have had a fight.

They may *de-escalate,* playing the roles for a while then getting bored and drifting off to something else, or realizing that things are not going in a healthy direction and stepping out of role.

Eric Berne referred to this kind of Drama, with two people playing complementary roles, as 'racketeering'.

However, what often happens is that at some point in the role-playing, one of the players throws a *Switch*. This is where things get really dark, and deserve a chapter of their own.

Drama: the Early Stages

Initiator

    Issues Game Invitation, either

    to the world at large (general)

    or to a specific individual (targeted)

Sucker

    Has 'hot button' which is pressed by the Invitation

    Buys in

    They've been 'hooked'

Pastimes

    Play with fellow players of the same role

Role Competition

    Also with fellow players of the same role...

    ...but this time, there's a competition to be best at it

With a Complement (someone playing a different role)

    'Racketeering'

    This can escalate (get more intense) or de-escalate

Or... Read on!

Chapter Seven

Acting Out the Roles 2: The Switch

The Switch is where the truest power of Drama lies.

The first dramas that we know were written in Ancient Greece. So were the first analyses of how Drama worked. The philosopher Aristotle (384 – 322 BC) outlined a number of concepts that Hollywood screenwriting gurus still use 2,300 years later. At the heart of Drama's narrative energy, he said, lay *Reversal*.

A Reversal is one of those moments when events appear to be heading in one direction but are suddenly revealed to be going somewhere very different. Reversals are the moments when the audience's whole understanding of the world of the story changes.

Any decent movie will have at least one of these. The protagonist's biggest ally turns out to be on the side of the baddies. The prime suspect in a murder mystery is found dead. A letter found in the love interest's pocket reveals that they are already in a relationship. The story pivots around, and is driven by, these.

These are exactly what Switches are. On the Drama Triangle, it comes when one of the people who has been playing one role *suddenly starts playing another one*. It is usually the initiator who does this, though this is not an infallible rule.

Story One, at the start of this book, had two main Switches. Chris started out as Persecutor, losing his temper, then switched to Rescuer by fixing the bikes – upon which Victim Emma suddenly switched to Persecutor, saying she wasn't interested in going for a bloody bike ride. In Story Four, the gun-toting Persecutor switched to Victim, turning the weapon on himself. The football coach, who attempted a Rescue, ended up as Victim.

Being Switched

Just like the best movie twists, the most powerful Switches come out of the blue. One moment someone is being aggressive, the next they are trying to please you. One moment they are being all helpless, the next they are putting you down.

The power of the Switch is that once you are on the Triangle playing a role with another person, when that person switches role, *you are psychologically compelled to change your role too. You* get switched. *You* get changed. *You* find yourself forced to play another of the roles.

This is the heart of Drama. This is what gives it its power, its intensity, its (for some people) addictive attraction.

Here are two examples from the world of dating.

One

A man finds a woman, fills her ears with flattery and her stomach with alcohol. They go back to his place and have sex. Then he switches, telling her to leave – he has important work to do tomorrow (unlike their unimportant relationship). He may even tell her how cheap she is.

Switched, she has to trudge home on what is known as 'the walk of shame'.

She has been put on the Triangle as a Rescuer, beautifying his world –

then he switches to Persecutor and she instantly becomes a Victim.

Two

A woman flirts with a man, flashes a bit of thigh (or a lot of thigh), which he then touches. She rounds on him and denounces him as a pig. She has come on as a Rescuer, fulfilling his needs, then switches to Persecutor and switches him to Victim.

I suspect that both the people who ended up as Victims in these stories found themselves muttering "Why does this always happen to me?"

What is going on?

The initiator, first. In TA theory, the motivation is that he or she ultimately gets to play the role they really want. Both the seducers in the dating stories above really want to play Persecutor.

So why don't they just go round persecuting people? Why all the preamble? The answer is that if you really want to play the role, you need a captive, willing partner. You could just go up to someone and start bullying them, but the chances are a) that they would protect themselves in some way, and b) that anyone watching would disapprove and might even step in and stop you. But if you get the person into a Triangle role first by appearing to meet a need of theirs, then you can – *at a time and place of your choosing* – switch to your preferred role and they will be psychologically unable not to complement you.

Bait. Entrap. Then, at the time that suits you best, switch.

Perpetrators of long-term domestic violence often appear to the world as pleasant and reasonable individuals, only switching to Persecutor when it is safe for them to do so.

TA theory says that the sucker subconsciously really wants to play the role they end up with, too. That explains the 'Why does this always happen to me?' reaction.

I fear this is often true. This awareness needs to be handled sensitively. It's easy to misuse it and say that the Victims in the two seduction stories have 'asked for it' in some way and so the inviter / switcher has no moral responsibility for what happened. People sometimes say the same about people in abusive relationships.

This book does not condone such judgements. Bullying, deceit, manipulation and violence are still bullying, deceit and manipulation and violence, even if the victim of these has a measure of subconscious complicity. If you hear this book – or the Drama Triangle generally – being used to justify unacceptable behaviour, this is a misuse of the model.

The message to anyone who is a Victim in an abusive relationship is to get help. If the help is to be effective, the Victim will have to take a hard, probably painful look at their own hot buttons and why they respond to them. Totally blaming the other person only switches to Persecutor and perpetuates the Drama. True strength is taking a clinical look at yourself, gaining self-knowledge from that, and changing – there's plenty of material on how to do that in the second half of this book. It's an achievement to get out of a destructive relationship, but the real win is making yourself wiser and stronger so that you never enter another one again. If this book can help people achieve such outcomes – well, that's why it was written. Not to justify bullies.

Let's return to less intense subject matter and analyze Story Three at the start of this book in the light of TA theory. Your colleague wanted to play Persecutor – it's their favourite role. But they have a reputation as a nice person to keep, so they don't want to swagger around looking for obvious Victims. Instead, they lured you onto the Triangle by playing Victim (remember, though we have favourite roles, we can play all of them). You were cast as Rescuer. In the next few interactions ('transactions' in TA terminology), they reinforced these roles, asking for help but instead of accepting the help, rejecting it in a Victim-y way, revealing ever more how desperate their situation was. This got you deeper into Triangle territory, ever more eager to Rescue this unfortunate person. When they felt you were really on board and really identified with your Rescuer role, they pulled the Switch – "You're no help!" At this point, they got what they wanted, to be playing their favourite, Persecutor role. And they did so in a way that didn't damage their public image as a nice, rather put-upon person, because you had 'asked for it' by offering 'useless' advice. You were left feeling strange, tricked, helpless – a Victim.

This may seem oddly devious, but that's the subconscious for you! It wants what it wants – in this example, to play Persecutor – and has been learning and refining strategies to achieve this goal since childhood.

The TA explanation of the bait / trap / switch process is powerful, but I believe that there are other reasons why people might want to play this game, too. This is deep material. I shall look at these reasons in Chapter Ten.

The Switch as Plan B (or C)

Sometimes initiators can switch before a Game Invitation gets accepted.

Keith gets angry with Paula over a relatively trivial matter. Subconsciously he hopes that will push her into Victim, after which he will be able to Rescue her. But Paula is used to dealing with his temper and simply lets him rant on.

After a while, his subconscious realizes that his invitation is being declined. So he suddenly switches to Victim, complaining that nobody ever listens to him, and how lousy his life is as a result. Paula, a kind-hearted soul, leaps in to the Rescue. Result! She is now on the Triangle. Keith can now take his time and find a way of switching her to Victim.

Maybe he'll belittle her attempts at Rescuing, like the person in Story Three. That will make her a Victim, whereupon he can leap onto his white horse and Rescue her, armour glinting in the sun as he does so.

The Immediate Consequences of the Switch

The first consequence of being switched is often simple shock. "What just happened?" "What did I do?"

Eric Berne referred to this moment as the 'Cross-up'. He said that it *always* followed Switches, but I'm not sure it always does.

As well as this mental confusion, a physical sense of disempowerment and exhaustion often follows being switched, too. This is hardly surprising. Basically, somebody has hacked into your emotional system and has messed with it.

The unhelpful and sometimes unpleasant emotions that go with the role you have been switched to will come to the fore, even though a minute ago you weren't feeling them at all. You'll feel all helpless and Victim-y, or angry and Persecutorish, or frustrated as an incompetent but well-intentioned Rescuer.

As this is all at the subconscious level, initiators may feel the same sense of shock, too. 'Why am I doing this?' their conscious minds will ask. They may even blame the sucker for what they have just done (the common Persecutor 'he/she was asking for it' justification is a classic example of this).

Games

The above is kind of interaction that Eric Berne called a 'Game'. He had a formula for it: a Game involved an Invitation, a buy-in, some playing of the initial roles, a Switch, a cross-up and payoffs to both participants of playing their favourite Triangle role.

He even made an ironic mathematical version:
$$C + G = R > S > X > P$$

C and G were 'con' and 'gimmick', Berne's words for Invitation and hot button. R was the buy-in, S the Switch, X the 'cross-up' and P the payoffs where both players, in his view, got to play the roles they subconsciously wanted.

S, the Switch, was the essence of the Game, however. That was the thing that made it so destructive.

I'm going to simplify his formula a little. There doesn't have to be a cross-up (though there often is). And do both players get what they subconsciously need? Again, probably they often do, but maybe this isn't always the case. To me, the defining essence of a Game is:

- An Invitation

- A hot button

- A buy-in

- (often) a few rounds of Triangle role-playing

- A Switch

- At least one player gets the outcome they subconsciously want.

Sagas

Games tend not to happen in isolation. In many situations where people are stuck with each other – in relationships, in institutions, in workplaces – people can act out long Dramas with loads of Switches. Chris and Emma's relationship (Story One) is one of these. The relationship lumbers on and on, with Switches from both participants at different times. I call these dismal affairs *Sagas*.

The plays of Alan Ayckbourn often feature such miserable stuff, with the Game-playing exaggerated for comic effect. The work of Mike Leigh also often digs into such sorry relationships.

In Sagas, players can take turns at initiating and at being the sucker. There can be periods of apparent normality, until one person gets bored and leaps onto the Triangle, inviting the other one to join them. (If the players have known each other for years, they will know each others' hot buttons perfectly.) Off they go again!

The TA hypothesis that Game initiators and suckers play Games because that ends up with them playing their favourite role doesn't always seem to apply to Sagas, as Saga participants keep switching, and ending up in different roles. However, a TA purist would say, "Ah, but they always *end up* in their favourite role."

Maybe.

Can Sagas ever end?

Of course, but not always well.

They can end very badly if the Games escalate. Chris and Emma bicker and Switch, but they don't escalate. Other couples do – hence domestic violence. I discuss levels of Drama in the next chapter.

More positively, one of the players may quit. Chris will come home one day to find that all Emma's clothes, books and CDs – plus the cat – have gone. There is a note lying on the table.

This would seem to be for the best. But who are they going to pair off with next? There's a pleasant, fair-minded bloke called Jaden at Emma's work. She thinks he's nice looking, but a bit wild. Maybe she could straighten him out a bit… Chris, as 'dumpee', may take a little while to start dating again, but will probably then find another woman to play the same Games with.

Or maybe one or both of them will grow and start sorting themselves out. There is always hope.

Other Sagas just rumble on, like one of those volcanoes that never actually erupts but which always has a sinister plume of smoke coming out of it. In the old days, when divorce was stigmatized and rare, many marriages ended up like this.

What a waste!

The Switch

The heart of Drama
    It has been for 2,300 years!

The scene begins…
    with both players on the Triangle, playing V,P or R

The Switch
    The initiator suddenly changes role
    This makes the sucker change role too
    For Berne, the Switch makes an interaction a 'Game'

Consequences
    The 'Cross-up'. "What the hell just happened?"
    The sucker (especially) feels disempowered and exhausted
    The initiator gets to play the Triangle role they desire…
    …in a way that keeps them appearing socially acceptable
    Maybe the sucker does, too

Sagas
    Interactions that contain a long series of Switches
    Also includes periods of ordinary behaviour
    Various possible endings…
    …or none

Chapter Eight

Degrees of Drama

This book started out with four stories, all of which involved Triangle roles and switching. Some were a lot more serious than others, however. Eric Berne talked about three different 'degrees' of Drama.

First degree Drama was the sort of thing that, once you have got over the initial embarrassment, you can laugh or shrug off later. The lighter (though still irritating) events of Story Three fall into this category.

Second degree involves the kind of embarrassment you really don't want to talk about. Botched seductions, rows between couples and falling for cons often fall into this category. Story One was one of these: neither Emma nor Chris would admit the goings-on to anyone else.

Third degree involves criminal activity and/or physical violence.

Berne lumped the taking of life in with this third degree, as an ultimate version of it. I regard this as a *fourth* degree.

Arguably there is a *fifth* degree, reserved for certain political leaders who actively promote violence and start wars.

Moving up the Ladder

I've already talked about how some players 'escalate' Drama by heightening the intensity or by dragging other people into the show, as the shooter did in Story Four. Full-on escalation means notching things up from one of the degrees above to the next. A Saga can begin with niggles and end in violence.

This kind of escalation may not be easy to predict, especially from the outside. This is because second-degree dramas are, by their nature, kept quiet (switching, remember, can be a way of getting socially unacceptable payoffs while appearing socially acceptable). As a result of this, third-degree dramas may appear to come out of nowhere. They've usually been quietly building up, however. Seen from outside, someone:

- acts 'a bit weird' (first degree)
- goes quiet – which appears to show they were quite 'normal' really (second degree)

then

- boom! (third degree)

Loyalty Points

Underlying the escalation is a simmering and growing pool of negative role-emotion – one or several of those learnt ones discussed in the Chapters Two, Three and Four (Eric Berne talked of 'favourite bad feelings').

Role-reinforcing memories are part of the schemas we build to shape and justify our role-playing. Keen Drama players will build a library of these. Berne used the metaphor of collecting 'trading stamps'. These were used to reward shoppers in the 1960s; you got them with each purchase, stuck them in a little book, and when you had enough you could trade them in for a usually rather tacky consumer item. A modern metaphor would be supermarket Loyalty Points.

The school shooter in Story Four would have had many experiences that built up his collection of Victim Loyalty Points. It might have begun with abuse in his childhood. School would no doubt have provided more. The onset of puberty offered points with each failure:

on the sports field, in class. Double points for failures with the opposite sex. Points could also be racked up at Victim sessions, listening to victimy songs or competing with other Victim players online to be the most persecuted and miserable. There would be Dramas with Switches, where he tried to Rescue or Persecute and ended up switching or being switched back to Victim. All the time, his collection of Loyalty Points was growing. Victim energy was gathering. Victim values were being confirmed. When he had all the points he needed, it was time to head down to the gun store and cash them all in.

Some people, sadly, are avid points collectors. But most of us don't escalate drama; we sometimes act out dramas at first or second level, but thankfully never ratchet them further. We don't like hoarding negative feelings. Life, we feel instinctively, is for living, not sitting around feeling angry or sad. We have ways of 'letting off steam'. We laugh stuff off where we can. We talk more serious things through with friends, families or therapists (or total strangers we meet in bars or on trains). We can look at ourselves and be gently critical.

Degrees of Drama

First

    You can laugh it off later

Second

    You won't talk about it to anyone else

Third

    Criminal or violent

Fourth

    Fatal

Fifth

    Successful propagandists for war or violence

Escalation

    More and more episodes
    Other people drawn in
    Moving up the ladder

'Loyalty Points'

    Hoarding negativity to justify escalation
    Some people 'cash them all in' at one extreme event
    But most of us don't…

        Life has a natural, positive call
        We have ways of letting off steam
        Old negativity often fades
        Our better selves won't let us

Chapter Nine

The Dramatic World

So far, I have looked at drama in all its manifestations as being internally driven. People do this stuff, I've said, because of their psychological make-up.

Some psychologists, however, argue that our behaviour is not internally driven but caused by our immediate environment. They are called 'situationists'. A scary experiment showed their views to be truer than we, in our individualistic age, like to think.

In 1971, psychology professor Philip Zimbardo thought he'd see how students – mainly nice, liberal-minded youngsters – reacted to being asked to play roles. He set up a prison, with some students acting as warders and others as prisoners. The warders had to keep order, even if the prisoners got bolshy.

I don't know if Zimbardo was influenced by the Triangle, which had emerged three years before. He certainly created a perfect way of getting people to play Persecutors and Victims.

Participants started embracing the roles with enthusiasm at once. After a few days, difficult 'prisoners' were being forced to defecate in buckets, sleep on bare floors or were locked in solitary confinement. The experiment had been planned to last a fortnight, but had to be terminated after six days as the students were behaving with unthinking cruelty and violence. A host of Triangle Dramas had been generated by the conditions and had quickly escalated.

Zimbardo's experiment shows that certain institutional set-ups nourish drama. The prison was an extreme version, as:

1. there was a huge, unbridgeable gap between the powerful and the powerless

2. rules had to be strictly and continually enforced

3. people couldn't get away, so a Drama that was interrupted for some reason could easily be picked up and resumed later.

The 'power difference' noted above can, I feel, extend to society as a whole. Research seems to show that highly unequal societies are more stressful than more unequal ones, and stress (more on this below) feeds Drama.

Cultures

Some cultures seem to nourish Drama. Millions of people tune into TV soap operas, with their endless Switches – the writers of these ought to pay Dr Karpman a royalty.

The old British boarding school was essentially a *Persecution Culture*. Bullying was rampant and accepted as 'character forming'. The more physical and psychological abuse kids could take, the tougher they would (in theory) become, so they could go out and build and run an empire with the required stoicism. If they became an emotional wreck in the process, well, that was collateral damage.

I've already discussed the modern *Victim Culture* (in Chapter Three).

Interestingly, in both cultures, a Switch soon gets pulled. Empire-building Brits switched to Rescuers. They told themselves that they had a mission to save 'savage' people from their 'savagery' and lead them towards the light of 'civilization'. The fact that the 'savages' hadn't asked for this help simply showed how much they needed it.

In the modern Victim culture, the offended (= Victim) internet-user soon switches to Persecutor, rushing, like Jez, to shame the latest individual who has made an 'inappropriate' post or comment. The online 'Incel' movement, which started as a kind of mutual consolation club for people who couldn't find sexual partners, turned into a Victim club where people spent most time moaning about the opposite sex rather than trying to cheer each other up. Then it switched, becoming a scary, misogynistic Persecutor club, with the ultimate result that some individuals went out and committed murders.

Rescuer cultures are often sub-cultures. They prevail in certain kinds of charity work, especially where there is a preponderance of volunteers. Well-intentioned volunteers can easily drift into being Rescuers – after which it is easy for them to switch to another triangle role. A friend got a dog from a benign-seeming animal rescue centre. She gave it a good home, but then someone from the centre decided it wasn't good enough, after which my friend was harassed by that individual, demanding the animal back. In the end, she had to get a lawyer to get this Rescuer-turned-Persecutor off her back. (The dog is still with her, by the way, loved and happy.)

The culture of the paid emergency services seems to include a brilliant dark, self-deprecatory humour that (usually) grounds these professional rescuers and stops them seeing themselves as mighty, noble Rescuers with a capital R.

Alongside these 'big' contexts, there are some less institutional, more temporary – but still often powerful – breeding grounds for drama. I shall list four of the most powerful ones below: stress, 'tricky topics', isolation and (I think, the most insidious) lack of clarity.

Stress

I'm not sure why stress makes us more susceptible to Drama, but I've seen it happen over and over again (and been in that position myself). Maybe it's because stress creates neediness, and neediness can inflame deeper pains – more on these in the next chapter.

What Drama doesn't do in stressful situations is help. At all. It just makes them worse. It creates more stress, which in turn makes us even more susceptible to Drama. A vicious circle of Drama and stress can spring up.

Tricky Topics

Some topics seem to create Drama: race, gender, homophobia, trans rights... 'Culture wars', often stirred up by politicians, are similar, especially where the issues revolve around identity. In the late 2010s, the UK split in two about leaving the European Union. If you wanted to ruin a British dinner party, mentioning 'Brexit' was the best way of doing it.

These big topics can be important – I'm not saying, 'Don't discuss them'. Far from it. But they can be fertile ground for Games and Switching. Sensible people will discuss these matters tactfully and objectively, in the light of this fact.

Isolation

The above causes are all social. I talked above about how being trapped in an intense institutional setting breeds Drama. Privacy, freedom from such settings, should liberate us from that pressure – and a decent measure of privacy clearly does. But *too much* isolation often puts the Drama back again.

Social media provide an excellent example of this. 'Social' in one sense, they are very un-social in another sense. Users sit alone at their computers for hours. The normal rules of human interaction can fade into the distance, and there aren't any actual humans around to remind users of those rules.

It can be the same in motor vehicles. We sit in our little worlds, battling with other little worlds. Few people barge into queues, but you don't need to spend long behind the wheel in a city before someone pulls out in front of you or – what a dark metaphor! – 'cuts you up'.

The perpetrators of terrible crimes – the ultimate in drama – often turn out to be 'loners'.

It is too early to tell the effects of the current 'lockdown' on people's psychology. Most of us seem to be handling it well, possibly because along with the lockdown there is a new sense of community, of facing a hideous external threat together. And thankfully, there are many communication media available to us.

It seems that somewhere between Zimbardo's hellish prison and the walled-off world of the psychological loner is a nice, healthy 'Low Drama Zone', where we have a reasonable balance between our own space and interaction with others.

Lack of Clarity
This is a major breeding ground for Drama – and often goes unnoticed, which is how it gets a lot of its power. There's nothing like invisibility!

Lack of clarity allows for the misunderstandings and misinterpretation of actions that lead to powerful Switches. It allows hidden agendas to remain hidden in the fog of unclearness, wating for the moment when they can – and will, even if we pretend they won't – leap out and yell 'Gotcha!' at us.

Lack of clarity can be individual. It can be people not saying what they want or being fuzzy about detail. Businessman Karl admits he's 'not a detail man'.

It can be institutional. "What are the rules round here?" Institutions often have 'unwritten' rules that newcomers are expected to pick up.

It can be cultural. All cultures come with expectations and unspoken norms. Some are more 'explicit' than others. In the Netherlands, you are expected to speak your mind. In China you are expected to preserve group harmony.

It can be informational. The rise of 'fake news' has created less certainty and clarity. Clear, accepted facts tend to repel Drama.

It can be social – what are the rules and expectations in a given situation? We've seen that the dating world is full of Game opportunities, and this is partially because the rules seem to be in a perpetual flux, from the grabby, macho 1970s to the prim world of contemporary PC. No doubt they vary from subculture to subculture, too.

Nik professes to despise social rules. He regards anyone who shows any sign of needing them as 'anal'. Odd how he often ends up getting in arguments…

Lack of clarity can hide behind big, often emotive generalizations, too. Rabble-rousing politicians are masters of this, bandying words like 'freedom' or 'equality' about without explaining what they mean, precisely, in practice. Freedom from what? When? Where? Equal in what respect?

Of course, it's not just politicians.

"You oppress me," Chris shouts at Emma one day.

"What the hell d'you mean by that?" she replies.

"You just tie me down with stupid little things I'm supposed to do!"

"Like what?"

"I don't know, just… things."

The vagueness of these terms gives power to the speaker, as the listener doesn't really know what he or she is on about. If the listener does try and 'unpack' them, the speaker can go into Victim and take this as an attack. Or they can Persecute: "God, you've got such a limited outlook you don't even know what 'freedom' means!"

Students of NLP will recognize the 'Meta Model' at work here.

External Causes of Drama

Institutional
> Big power gap
> Rules that have to be strictly enforced
> No escape

Culture
> Culture 'sets the tone'
>> Persecutor cultures – Brit boarding schools
>> Victim cultures – common today
>> Rescuer cultures – e.g. the overzealous animal lover

Stress
> The Vicious Circle
>> More stress, more drama, even more stress

'Tricky Topics'

Isolation
> Online or on four-wheels

Lack of Clarity
> By an individual
>> Who won't say what they want
>> Who won't go into detail
>> Who uses vague generalizations...
>> ... and refuses to 'unpack' them
> In a social situation
>> What are the expectations?
>> No rules

Chapter Ten

Why?

The Deep Ingredients of Drama

At our deepest psychological level, why do we do Drama (and why do some people do it more than others)?

I've left this question to this late in the book, as I feel it is best answered with an understanding of what Drama is and how it works.

I have already suggested some answers.

In Chapters Two, Three and Four, I looked at how people are *taught* Drama.

For some psychologists, that's the answer. People who do the most Drama are people who have been taught it the most often, the most clearly, the most forcefully. This is the kind of answer one would get from 'social learning theorists', who believe that our actions are the products of what we learn.

A contrary answer comes in Chapter Nine above. 'Situationists' believe it's the current situation that causes people to do Drama, driving them to it because things are unclear or oppressive (or both) or because Drama is rewarded in some way.

A third answer: TA argues that people do Drama because they

subconsciously want to play a particular role. This raises the question of why they want to play it, and I'll discuss this below. There's also, from TA, the notion that people hoard negative emotions till they suddenly explode in action – cashing in your Loyalty Club points. Again, this makes us ask why people do this – more on this below, too.

So which of these answers is right?

I don't know for sure – and nor does anybody else – but my strong sense is that none of them is, on its own, but that all of them are, as contributory parts of a story, as ingredients of a recipe for Drama.

Human beings are, above all, complicated; we are the products of our genes, our very early experiences, our later experiences, our beliefs, our values, our memories, where we are now – and our choices. 'Cause' in human affairs is a complex matter, building up over time.

In this chapter, I want to look at more of the deep ingredients of Drama.

Control and Power

In the chapters on the three Triangle roles, I said that one of the payoffs to each role was the control it can, in its own special way, help the player exert over other people.

But that is just the start of the controlling power of Drama.

Control grows when you stop simply playing the role and start actively *suckering other people* onto the Triangle. Initiators, remember, effectively take over suckers' motivational systems. They determine who the sucker thinks him- or herself to be ('I'm the meanest sonofabitch in town.' 'I'm a helpless Victim.' 'I must leap onto my white horse, charge in and sort this out.') They determine the images and memories running in the sucker's mind. How's that for power?

Switching takes the control to an even higher level. Not only has the initiator manipulated another person into a very specific particular mental state, but he or she has now made that person change to another, totally different mental state – in an instant. "Just watch me!" Click! "Suddenly the person I got playing Victim is now trying to Rescue everybody! And when I've had enough of that, I'll make them a Victim again. Or maybe get them all worked up as a Persecutor... I'm in charge!" (Well, 'I' the whole human being is not in charge; 'I' the Drama-addicted ego is in charge, of both players.)

In Sagas, the link between Drama and power can be incredibly forceful. What the initiator uses here is *unpredictability*.

"I never understand where I am with him," says Bella of her partner, Bob. "One moment he's loving and affectionate, the next cold and really quite unpleasant. I spend so much time worrying what he'll do next. I'm forever adjusting my behaviour, either to suit his latest mood, or to anticipate the next one. He keeps me on my toes all the time."

That last phrase, 'all the time', is particularly telling. People who excel in using Switches to control others keep them coming, so the 'switchee' never has time to step out of the Drama and get some perspective.

A while ago, Bella recently announced she was going to stay with her mum for a few days 'to straighten her head out'. An hour or so later Bob hit his thumb with a hammer fixing a curtain rail – something she'd been asking him to do for months – and was in such pain that she felt she couldn't leave him.

When his thumb got better, she said she was now going away – and he turned around and accused her of being selfish and scrounging off him (a few years ago, she gave up work because he said she didn't need to: he brought in enough money for two).

Bob is using Switching for control. Until Bella understands this and – this is the difficult part – her own partial complicity in this, she will never get out of this trap.

The ultimate power game is warfare, and the value of surprise (a.k.a. Switching) has been at the heart of military thinking for millennia. Back in 500 BC the Chinese strategist Sun Zi wrote, 'Let your plans be as dark and impenetrable as night, and when you move, fall like a thunderbolt.' A perfect motto for the Game-playing control-seeker.

Energy Theft

This is an odd kind of power play.

Some drama initiators fizz with energy. You wonder 'where they get it all from', until you spend some time with them, come away exhausted and conclude that, in the last hour or so, they have got it from you.

How do they do this? I'm not quite sure. (If you do have a theory, please let me know!) But I've seen it happen a lot.

Former England Rugby coach, Sir Clive Woodward has a term for these people: 'Energy Sappers'. He learnt it when he sent his team to train with the UK's elite Royal Marines. After the training, Woodward received a blunt assessment from a Marines sergeant major, who used that term to describe some of his individually most able players. The Energy Sappers were negative influences, the soldier said They criticised, belittled, undermined and, above all, blamed others – any mistake was always someone else's fault. They couldn't take any kind of criticism. He added that he would never go into battle alongside these people.

Attention

Drama can attract a lot of this, and some people love attention.

Yes, perpetrators of domestic violence will choose a private place to Switch, so as to minimize others' attention and keep up their respectable public image. But other Game players want the world to see. In Story Four, the shooter chose a very public place to show everyone what a Victim he was and how that Persecutory bitch – and women in general, and life in general – had driven his innocent Victim self to the edge. He probably also reckoned he'd get onto national news. The whole cruel world would learn about his martyrdom.

But even the most private Switcher gets a lot of attention – from one person, the sucker. After you've been baited, trapped and switched, you will drag the memory round with you for a while, like a horrible itch or a tune you can't get out of your head. Rather than going for mass attention, the switcher has made sure they got the undivided attention of one person: you.

Excitement

Drama, Switches and Sagas can simply liven up things for people who are bored.

One of the United fans in the pub confesses: "When I feel that desire to fight those scum [the other team's supporters], I feel really alive. The rest of my life is pretty f***ing boring."

Sherry says: "I admit it. I like to make a bit of a scene. It gives me a buzz. It shows people care. I can't stand all this polite dullness."

Given the amazing number of interesting things that exist in the world, it's worth asking why these people are so bored.

The Intimacy Eddy and the Intimacy Whirlpool

Eric Berne believed that the desire for 'intimacy' with others was a key human drive. He was often unclear on what he meant by this, but later thinkers in TA have interpreted the concept as 'connection at as many levels as possible'. Stephen Karpman's words are that intimacy with someone occurs when the various sides to your personalities are mutually 'experienced and welcomed'. It is when you can be open, truthful and spontaneous with someone and they can be the same with you.

There's a complex relationship between Drama and intimacy. Drama can sometimes be a rather inept attempt at intimacy. At other times it can be the opposite, an attempt to avoid intimacy.

The above paragraph might seem contradictory and unhelpful – but these two apparently opposite motivations can work alternately to form a perpetual loop, which I call the Intimacy Eddy.

Drama in search of intimacy. The Triangle roles can appear to be safe, familiar ways of presenting ourselves to others and getting some kind of reaction out of them.

They can give us a club to belong to. Back at The Duke's Head pub in Chapter Six, all three sets of pastimers felt close to each other because they shared playing a role.

Playing different roles can bring people together, too. Ettie, whose 'little emergencies' in Chapter Four kept carer Maria on her toes, was basically lonely. Her 'Victim' moments that got Maria Rescuing created contact for her.

"My husband and I have awful rows some time," says Melissa. "But that means we know each other better. We've seen each other at our worst — and here we are, still together." When the couple drift apart, they use rows to get communicating again.

Drama as an antidote to intimacy. Berne may have argued that intimacy is something we strive for, but it can also be something we fear. Do we really want to fully reveal ourselves to others? *All* of ourselves? What will they think? If we have been round a cycle of revelation and rejection (which most of us have if we've been in a close relationship that has gone wrong), then *avoiding* intimacy and its potential pain can become an important goal.

Sheila is terrified of being revealed as being weak and worthless — a judgement she made about herself as a child and which she confirmed when her first real love affair went wrong. She is, of course, really just a normal human being, a mix of strengths, imperfections and past mistakes like the rest of us, but she has decided that the world would rip her to shreds if it really knew her. So she does all she can to keep that world at bay.

Playing one of the roles can be a great way of doing that. Sheila had good Victim training as a child, so that role comes easily to her. It can irritate the hell out of anyone who gets too close.

André had excellent Persecutor training as a child, and as an adult has ended many relationships by suddenly getting angry and shouting at whoever it was threatened to get too close.

If these initial role-plays don't work, a Switch ought to scare most people off. Victim Sheila can try switching to 'passive aggressive'. André has a neat switch to overly apologetic Victim. These usually do the trick and drive away anyone who wasn't repelled by the first round of role-playing.

So here we have two reactions to intimacy: desire for it and fear of it. Being human, we can feel both: the subconscious has many mutually uncomprehending sub-units and these can be at war with each other. Part of us fears isolation. Another part fears rejection because we have revealed too much of ourselves.

Drama appears to help us buy off these two powerful parts of ourselves by appealing first to one, then to the other, then to the first one again, then to the second (and so on, for ever if 'necessary'). If we're lonely, Drama can attract some attention. If the attention gets too intense, we can use Drama to fend the attracted person off. "Get close – but not *too* close."

This makes Drama sound rather handy – but of course it's no long-term solution for either fear. We just go round and round, seeking intimacy then fending it off, then feeling lonely and seeking intimacy again, then feeling threatened and backing off, then feeling alone again… The Intimacy Eddy.

Because it's subconscious, of course, we don't even have a clue what's going on or why. We get used to this. "That's life…"

Mo is a charming guy. He attracts people (great!) but always seems to end up alienating them. He says this is OK – there are always more people out there to attract. But deep down, he is not happy about this. Nothing in his life lasts…

If the Drama escalates, the Eddy can turn into a Whirlpool, sucking players down into destruction. But usually it doesn't. Instead, many people just stay in their Eddy, polite but disconnected, going round and round and round and…

Much, much better to take control of their lives by understanding what's going on, and facing up to their fears of both loneliness and intimacy.

Drama and Identity

'Who am I?' is a question that hits many people in adolescence.

If we don't find a satisfactory answer, it can keep niggling away for the rest of our lives.

Role-playing can appear to provide an answer. Not, maybe, a conscious, verbal one – "I'm a Persecutor!" – but a feeling of rightness, of sensing that our role-playing behaviour is a genuine expression of who we really are. If we spent years being trained in the art of playing a role, playing it now will feel deeply 'right' in some way. I believe, of course, that we are more than that – but there will be times when a favoured role does feel like the answer to the 'identity question'.

When we 'pastime', performing our favourite role alongside others, we are effectively joining a Role Club. Club membership can be a powerful source of identity.

B, who we met briefly in Chapter Two, says, "Before I joined the gang I was nobody." The gang is a Persecutor Club.

Groups of people gathering to have a good moan can become Victim Clubs. Jo-beth joined a Victim Support Group after a particularly horrible break-up. Initially she found it supportive, but the culture in it has changed recently. "It used to be much more positive," she says, "but now people just sit around competing to be the biggest Victim."

Rescuers are usually more solitary, but can also form clubs. The small group of goodies out to save the world (often from a lone but utterly villainous Persecutor) is a staple fare of popular fiction.

I've already said that I don't believe that acting out Triangle roles is an expression of our truest, most profound selves. But when we are stressed, lost and confused – as most of us are at some times in our lives – a taught role, with its familiar feelings and free membership of a Role Club, can feel very authentic.

Our identity can also be seen as an expression of our *boundaries*. It's often said that growing up is a process of finding out where 'we' end and 'out there' begins. Part of this involves prodding the world to find out. "Can I have one more sweet? Ple – eeeease." Drama in Adults can be seen as part of our continuing prodding of the world to find boundaries.

Claudia is endlessly nosey about other people's affairs.

Ed is forever interrupting other people's conversations.

Stella is perpetually 'dropping in' on people, whether it suits those other people or not. When she has a formal appointment, she is often late for it.

Iqbal often 'mind reads', assuming that he knows what others are thinking and acting on these totally untested assumptions. He expects others to read his mind, too. He sometimes tells his wife Zaina, "You should know what I want!" When he wants to play Persecutor, he has the line "If you really loved me, you'd know what I want" ready. This line is itself a Switch, starting off as Victim (the implication of the first part is that Zaina doesn't really love him) then switching to the Persecutor implication that she should damn well know his mind. Games can play out very fast.

All the people above have 'boundary issues'. I suspect that, deep inside, some of them don't feel they are entitled to any space at all. But another part of them won't accept this (remember, the subconscious can be a battleground between mutually uncomprehending sub-systems). This part keeps prodding, prodding, prodding to disprove the self-denying one. Those prods often take the form of Game Invitations.

Drama and Narcissism: 'The Emotional Black Hole'

There are people out there who seem to have both a boundless egotism and an incredibly thin skin. They exude brashness and confidence, saying what they like about other people, but the moment anyone says anything remotely critical about them, they snap back with a hurt, vicious riposte. This is classic Switching from Persecutor to Victim then back to Persecutor again.

Psychologists call these people *narcissists*, citing the myth of the Greek youth who fell in love with his own reflection in a pond. Narcissists are not only in love with their reflection, but blind to everything else – probably because, deep down, they are terrified of everything else and its destructive power.

How do they get like this? Nobody knows. A common theory is that narcissism is a response to a trauma in very early life, where the individual felt that they were going to be annihilated. It doesn't have to be an actual threat: a perceived threat, such as an infant waking up and feeling abandoned, can be enough. The narcissist is forever seeking assurance that they haven't been (or aren't just about to be) obliterated.

This seeking is relentless: narcissists are the emotional equivalent of those black holes in space that suck everything within range into themselves. Drama goes hand in hand with narcissism. Narcissistic people are forever acting out Dramas of acceptance and rejection. "I though you were my friend, but you betrayed me." "I thought you were my friend, but you didn't come up to my standards."

Psychologists argue about whether we all have a bit of narcissism in us, or if it is a pathology just found in a smaller number of individuals. I'm inclined to the former view. Infancy is a time of intense emotions, positive and negative. I suspect that most of us carry some damage from that time.

This leads neatly onto the next explanation…

The Life Script

Eric Berne believed that Drama comes as a result of acting out what he called a 'Life Script'.

He argued that we write ourselves a Life Script to answer questions such how we find love, who we are, and how to make sense of the world around us: how life works, what really matters, who the good guys and the bad guys are, what happens to good guys and bad guys…

Berne believed that we do this aged around five. We then store the Script in our subconscious, from where it exercises a powerful but hidden influence. We find ourselves compelled to act it out, as adults, even though we are no longer consciously aware of its existence or contents. Drama is how we do this.

Life Scripts can be deeply dysfunctional, because we write them at an age when our thinking is still 'magical' – think of the fairy stories that enchant us at that time (especially the dark, surreal originals, not the sanitized, modern, 'PC' retellings). Five-year-olds can come to the conclusion that they can only be loved if they suffer, or if they are invisible, or, in the most extreme versions, if they kill for a cause or die (death is not the end in magical thinking).

Berne made this the lynchpin of his therapeutic model, arguing that *all* Drama was driven by our unconscious need to act out our Life Script and that 'script cure' was the ultimate aim of therapy.

This seems excessive. Yes, we all know or know of individuals whose lives come to dramatic ends and where we feel that, looking back, that end was inevitable. "He had it coming to him," said a classmate of the school shooter in Story Four after the event. In the ancient Greek tragedies watched by Aristotle, heroes and heroines are dragged down by a fate they are condemned to carry round with them, try as they might to put it aside. In the modern world, the beautiful but unfortunate Princess Diana always seemed to me to have some of this daemon in her.

However, most of us don't live like that. Some of us are highly successful, and most of us get by. If we do flirt with tragedy, it is when we are young and inexperienced, and our near-disasters are more the result of curiosity, sensation-seeking and ignorance than the impulsion of destiny. Older and wiser, we avoid such extremes rather than hurtle towards them with ever-increasing intensity.

Berne ingeniously got round this objection by saying that there are different kinds of Life Script. Some people have written themselves *winning* scripts, whereby they have happy and fulfilled lives. Others have written themselves a *banal* script, where they don't achieve the things they desire but muddle along OK. The people I described earlier in this chapter as being 'bored' with life would have written themselves such scripts, according to Berne's theory. They would have schemas which included maxims like 'Don't get too enthusiastic about anything – you'll make yourself look silly.' It is people with a third kind of script, a *losing* one, who are compelled to act out Drama.

There are interesting links between Berne's idea and 'attachment theory'. Since the 1950s, psychologists have been examining how we form attachments as infants, and how this affects our later relationships. John Bowlby, arguably the leading figure in this field, believed that the effect was massive: our attachment to our 'caregiver' (usually our mother) is our first intense emotional relationship, and he claimed that it set the pattern for all our future ones, via what he called an 'Internal Working Model'. The Life Script sounds pretty like this.

Mary Ainsworth, a pupil of Bowlby's, developed this idea. She created an observational technique called the 'strange situation', a scripted (for the adults) role-play involving an infant, its mother and a stranger. In essence, the infant is abandoned by its mother (briefly), comforted by the stranger, then mum returns. From watching many of these interactions, Ainsworth concluded that there were three essential types of attachment:

- Secure. Mother and child have bonded well. In the 'strange situation', the child gets upset when mum leaves, but when she returns, all is soon well again. (The good news is that in studies round the world, over half the infants observed showed secure bonding, or 'secure enough' bonding, to have taken place.)
- Insecure / Avoidant. The bonding has been partial. The child under-reacts to the events in the 'strange situation', not that fussed if mum leaves and not that bothered about the presence of the stranger, either.
- Insecure / Resistant. Also a result of inadequate bonding, but in this case the infant flips between clinginess to mum and a sudden rejection of her on her return.

'Insecure / Resistant' attachment sounds very much like Switching.

Ainsworth's three types of attachment map neatly onto Berne's three types of Life Script. Is a winning script a response to Secure attachment, a banal script a response to Insecure / Avoidant attachment, and a losing script – the kind that gets people to do lots of Drama – a response to Insecure / Resistant attachment?

The theory that Drama comes from a subconscious Life Script, written in response to the experience of attachment is a fascinating one, on which I'd like to see more research. It could be married to the 'social learning' and 'situationist' approaches:

- The experience of poor attachment leaves us with trauma...

- ...which we come to terms with (in a 'magical' way) via a Life Script that is, in reality, destructive.

- The Script requires us to act out Drama; our upbringing teaches us which of the three Triangle roles to prefer (and how to be expert at them)

- In adult life, particular situations draw out these preferences and turn them into Game Invitations and Switches...

Would such a theory turn out to explain everything? I doubt it. For one thing, we all have some propensity to slip into Drama, so if Berne's theory is right, we must all have a losing script tucked away somewhere. The more fortunate majority of people must have other stories and other motivations that outshout it.

I hope this chapter has been helpful. I'd love to reveal a simple formula – "Drama is caused by one thing and one thing only, and here it is!" But I can't. People are too complex.

The closest I can get is to point out a *theme* running through these causes of Drama – a theme, not a unique, ultimate cause. This theme is a sense of despair about human interaction. Author and philosopher Jean-Paul Sartre once said (or at least had a character in one of his plays say) "Hell is other people." This sense pervades the worlds we have visited in this chapter. Control freaks crave power because they are secretly terrified that uncaring, malevolent others will control them.

The attention-seeker fears that others will abandon them. In the Intimacy Eddy we crave connection then are repelled by it. The identity seeker is haunted by meaninglessness, by not knowing who they are or how they fit into the world. The narcissist weaves these fears into a web of delusion, of self and others. In Berne's theory, people with a 'losing' Life Script have written some or all of these terrors into a story that they are then compelled to act out and make real – possibly because they failed to bond well enough with their first caregiver.

Ouch!

Fortunately, there are remedies for all these painful ways of experiencing and living in the world. We can challenge Drama on many fronts. Some approaches will work well for some people, others for others. We need to create our own recipe for ditching Drama. How we do that is what the rest of this book is about.

Why?

Past Learning

The Current Situation

Control and Power

      Just playing the role gives power (see Chapters 2 – 4)

      Getting someone onto the Triangle gives more power

      And then you switch them!

          Keeping other people 'perpetually on their toes'

      'Energy Theft'

Attention and Excitement

The Intimacy Eddy

      Loneliness is horrible

          Drama can initiate contact

      Too much revelation can be terrifying

          Drama can put up a wall

      We eddy round and round between these two fears

A Manifestation of Narcissism

      Perpetual picking up then 'dropping' of individuals

Identity Needs

      Familiar feelings: 'This is who I am'

      Boundaries: still testing where our reality ends

Berne's Life Script Theory

      Written when we are too young to understand life

      Stored in the subconscious

      Three types: winning, banal, and losing

      Probably related to early 'attachment' (or failure to attach)

Despair: a Common Theme

Chapter Eleven

Get out! Avoiding Drama Before it Starts

There we have it: Drama; how it hooks into us; various possible reasons why it does so with so much power. So what do we *do* to move beyond it, to get it out of our lives? In the next few chapters I'll look at various answers.

I shall begin with an emergency procedure. If you realize that you are in the early stages of a Drama, how do you spot it and get out before a Switch takes place?

I have a model called Drama DEFCON. The idea comes from the US military, who look at the world situation and classify it by degrees of threat. They have various 'defense readiness conditions' or DEFCONs, starting with 'situation normal' (Level Five) and ending up with 'imminent war' (Level One).

It might seem a little flippant to use this as a metaphor for spotting some upcoming psychological mischief at a dinner party. Maybe it is, but it works. (It also introduces an element of irony into the proceedings, which in itself can help deflate egos and thus the situation.)

Drama DEFCON Five is, like the military's, 'situation normal'. Life just going on. You're pretty much in control of things, and the people around you are the same. Everyone has a pretty clear idea of what they need to do and what the rules are.

Sadly, many lives are lived at the next Drama DEFCON Level, or even at higher ones.

Is the environment stressful? Are emotions to the fore? Is there a lot of emphasis on status and power, and are there massive inequalities in the distribution of that status and power? Is judgement being passed on someone? Is there a lack of clarity about what's going on? Are there rules you (or other people) don't understand? Does everybody have the information they need? Is someone hiding something? Raise the level to Drama DEFCON Four.

Do you get a 'bad feeling' about a particular individual? Don't damn them out of hand – such impressions can be false – but raise the level to Drama DEFCON Three.

Is anyone out there playing a Triangle role? Is someone coming on aggressively, or acting all Victim-y, or getting ready to charge in and Rescue? Raise the level to Drama DEFCON Two.

Do you feel a rising, emotion-driven desire to respond to how that person is behaving? Do you get the sense of one of your 'hot buttons' suddenly crying out to be pressed? The more you think about what's in this book, the better you'll be at spotting moments like these. You'll start to notice inner signals, like speech patterns in your internal dialogue and physical feelings in particular parts of your body, that show you are in danger of leaping onto the Triangle.

Red alert! Drama DEFCON One!

Drama DEFCON

<u>Five</u>
Situation normal

<u>Four</u>
The situation has unusual potential for Drama

      Stress

      Status, power, guilt and blame are issues

      Expectations, rules (etc.) are unclear

      There's someone around who you know likes Drama

<u>Three</u>
You feel uneasy about someone

<u>Two</u>
Someone is playing a Triangle role

<u>One</u>
You feel a strong temptation to Persecute, Rescue or play Victim

I've assumed in the model above that you are the sucker (just as the military see themselves as defenders, not aggressors). But we can all initiate Drama, too. In such cases, our Level Three is about spotting a potential sucker. We then leap straight to Level One.

In Sagas, participants like Chris and Emma are pretty much permanently at Drama DEFCON Four. Things can jump very quickly to Level Three, when one participant 'seems to be in a funny mood', and the further, to when the Drama begins.

All of the levels have implications for action. Don't panic if you feel levels rising – do something!

Level Five.
Value this state of affairs, and do all you can to keep things this way!

Level Four.
Take extra precautions to remain calm. Remind yourself of the material in this book, especially how Drama is easy to slip into and the damage it can cause.

Try a simple mindfulness technique like deep breathing. Make a resolution to stay 'grown up' and not get into any Games.

Try and establish as much *clarity* as you can, for yourself and everyone else. What are the rules? What is the purpose of whatever is going on? Do you need information you don't have? Can you get hold of it? Does everybody else have the information they need? Can you help them get it (without obviously Rescuing them from their ignorance)? If a discussion is going on, what are the facts?

Level Three.
Make a quiet mental note of your intuitive perception. Be more guarded about how you deal with this individual, but otherwise carry on as normal. To put too much attention onto a possible Game player is to begin to put yourself into their hands (and into the hands of your own inner sucker).

Level Two.
Now is a good time to go through those Level Four activities again, but with greater urgency and intensity. Remind yourself of your earlier resolution to stay 'grown up', and make extra effort to put it into practice.

If at all possible, take control of the situation and lead it back to more solid ground (more on this below).

Level One.

Remove yourself from the situation. Physically if possible, internally if not. Then try and reconnect with your 'Inner Adult': reasonable, rational, fair-minded, equal.

Looking at some of these manoeuvres in greater detail...

Mindfulness and Breathing

Concentrate your attention onto something. The classic object is your own breath. Take deep breaths – itself a good antidote to the emotional stirring up that almost always surrounds Drama. As you take these breaths, pay attention to the process of doing so.

We don't normally attend to our breathing – it's one of those jobs that the subconscious just gets on with. Now notice it. Different teachers suggest attending to different aspects. I prefer breathing through the nose and feeling the breath passing in and out. Others recommend feeling the breath going deep down into your lungs.

Another mindfulness technique is to focus your attention onto a simple external object like a pen on the table or a picture on the wall (not a person, as this is too distracting).

Try these now. First, five slow, deep breaths. Then rivet your attention on an everyday object for fifteen seconds.

In both exercises, you may find your mind flipping from the object of your attention to 'concentrating on concentrating'. Totally random thoughts may enter your mind. Try and observe these interruptions rather than either engaging with them or actively trying to shoo them away. Meditation teachers use the image of standing quietly on a hill watching clouds pass.

Naturally, in an actual situation, these exercises can only be brief – it will not impress anyone if you go into a meditative trance in the middle of a crucial meeting. However, if you regularly practice meditation in quiet times, away from stress, you will find it easier to flip quickly and briefly into this state when you need to.

Staying 'Grown up'

Eric Berne talked of three 'ego-states'. Having been trained in the Freudian tradition, he used the word 'ego' in a neutral sense, meaning mindset, rather than the negative meaning we use it today, to describe our most selfish, entitled side.

The three states were 'Parent', 'Adult' and 'Child'. The first and the third states are both legacies of childhood. 'Parent' is full of maxims handed down by parents and behaviours and moods copied from them. 'Child' is how we felt and thought as children. Drama is almost always acted out from one of these two states.

'Adult' is different. I shall say more about it in Chapter Fifteen. Right now, just note that it's the state to be in when the Drama DEFCON scale begins to creep up.

Taking Control

If a conversation is going on, steer it out of the rut it is in. Lead it towards facts not feelings, towards possible courses of action not moral judgements. Cut out any emotionally laden words. If the other person keeps heading in this direction, don't go there with them.

Have lines ready for this. "I don't feel this is going in the right direction." "Can we get back to...?" "X is a rather emotionally laden word; I'd rather describe such people as Y." You may even recall the moment you found yourself hooked in – can you get back to what was being discussed at that moment, and lead the conversation back to that point then on in a new, more rational direction?

This can be done without confrontation. Consider, for a moment, that the other person is not in a really good place: what they are doing is inauthentic and probably motivated by old, past 'stuff'. Smile at them, at least briefly, as you lead them, politely but firmly, away from the Triangle to an adult interaction.

If the other person has read this book, cite it. "Are we getting into a Game here?"

Get Out!

If you find yourself at Drama DEFCON One, *simple physical escape* is the best option. If you are in a formal situation, you can't just rush out of the door – but can you go and get a glass of water or say you need to go to the loo? Anything to buy time and space. Masters of the art of issuing Game Invitations try and deny potential suckers time and space. Don't let them!

If you really can't remove yourself physically in any way, disengage from any ongoing conversation. 'Just going quiet' is better than boiling over. Better still to have lines like "I need time to think about that" or "I can't really reply to that just now".

Can you at least take one physical step back? One pace away from whoever is generating the aggro is one pace towards safety and choice.

Get out internally. Do what NLP practitioners call 'breaking state'.

- Look away – at the corner of the room or out of the window.

- Change your stance. If you sense you are being pushed into Victim, straighten yourself up, tall and proud. If you sense you are heading towards Persecutor, loosen up. Get 'easy' and relaxed. The same goes if you suddenly feel the urge to Rescue: loosen up, relax.

Develop your own ways of 'inner escape'. Elizabeth says, "When faced with a difficult person, I imagine an invisible but protective wall between them and me. I think of things bouncing off it: comments, prejudices, unpleasant thoughts. I know that sounds a bit weird, but it works really well!"

Jeff: "If I can tip my palm up, a kind of mini-version of holding out a hand in a 'stop' gesture, I do that. It feels like I've done the full gesture like a policeman stopping traffic, but actually it's just a tiny movement most people won't notice."

Drama DEFCON: What to Do

Five

Situation normal

> Enjoy the normality and the absence of Drama!

Four

The situation has unusual potential for Drama

> Remind yourself of Drama's allure but destructiveness
> Remind yourself of the Drama DEFCON model
> Use mindfulness techniques
> Resolve to stay 'grown up'
> Establish as much clarity as possible

Three

You feel uneasy about someone.

> Note, but don't overreact

Two

Someone is playing a Triangle role

> Re-run the Level Four activities, with more seriousness
> Take control and lead back to solid ground

One

You feel a strong temptation to play a complementary role

> Get out!
> Physically if possible, mentally if not

Chapter Twelve

Get over it! Getting on with Life after a Switch

Supposing these doesn't work, or you don't realize you're in a Game until too late? The Switch gets pulled. Ouch!

Get away

Yes, you should have done this earlier, but the best thing is still to get out. Physically if you can, internally if you can't. Try and reconnect with your inner Adult as soon as possible (see Chapter Fifteen).

The *worst* thing to do is to start another round of Drama. Especially if that involves escalating.

Among insecure young men, who are playing the Persecutor role because they think it's tough (and that they have to be tough to matter), extreme violence can grow from a tiny insult via a series of escalating reprisals. If you are in such a spiral of escalation, don't feel your honour will be compromised if you get out. It won't be. It will be increased.

Jason: "I suddenly realized this argument was stupid and going nowhere. When I first backed down part of me felt ashamed, like I'd chickened out. But I soon realized I'd done myself a favour. I was being the grown-up one, the strong one."

Don't try and get the last word. Experienced Drama initiators are masters at doing this, and *you will not beat them*. Even if you suddenly come up with what feels like a killer put-down, they will have heard it before, and will have a response ready that will hook you straight back onto the Triangle again.

More likely, you will think of that brilliant put-down a while after the Switch. If you are no longer in the initiator's company, you will be consumed with the desire to go back and shout it at them. (The French talk about *esprit d'escalier*, that brilliant comment you think of on the staircase down from the Paris apartment you have just left.) Don't. Just carry on trudging down the staircase. Later you'll feel proud of having risen above the temptation.

Don't leap into Rescuer mode, either. Kate says, "After one of these horrible game things, I find myself feeling sorry for this person. They can't have much of a life if they alienate people the way they alienated me. And then I find myself thinking, they really need help. I could provide it!"

Maybe you could help them, but you are not their therapist, and this is not the time. Right now, you have to get out and get yourself back together again. If the person is a family member or close colleague, then you can think about helping them later. Try now and you'll do it wrong and invite another foray onto the Triangle.

Deal with the Mess
Once you have got away physically, you will still be trapped mentally, irked by the annoyance (or worse) of having been lured onto the Triangle and switched.

Distraction can help. This person has inserted themselves into your mind with their game-playing. Don't let them have the run of it. Find something else to concentrate on. Ideally, it should be something that

111

requires adult reason and effort. If it involves researching some new stuff all the better – let your curiosity loose in a different world.

If you can, *talk* about the episode with a friend or your partner. In finding words to describe what happened, you may suddenly gain a new understanding (quite how this happens is a wonderful mystery). And the views of a third party can often bring a great blast of clarity and normality to a situation. Sometimes, this can be along the lines of "Typical X! They always do that", which can make you feel a lot better.

My wife understands TA, so I just say, "I got into a Game the other day…" and she knows what I mean. With someone who doesn't know this stuff (give them this book for Christmas!), just begin with "Something weird happened the other day…"

It is by definition a lot harder to talk about Second Degree games. You need a high level of trust and mutual respect to do this. Or talk with a therapist – something you definitely need to do, as a matter of urgency, if the game was Third Degree.

Heal. We are designed to get over stuff. However, this can be a bumpy ride. The brain has a natural rubbish-clearance system, but it isn't perfect. You will find yourself suddenly recalling this nasty business, and wincing as you do so.

Understand that 'unwanted recalls' happen, and that when they do that doesn't mean that the Drama has won, after all.

Change often takes place in a 'sawtooth' – two steps forward, one step back. The step back can hurt. In those moments of backsliding, remind yourself that these moments are part of a bigger, ultimately healing process. Keep working on ditching your Drama, and move on upwards again.

Make it Better

Once you are calm and yourself again, you *may* be able to do something to cancel out whatever Triangle position you ended up on. This is not the same as getting your own back or escalating.

If you ended up Persecuting, apologise. No need to tell the whole story, and don't try to justify. Just a nice simple, "I lost my cool there. I'm sorry." Not "Sorry I lost my cool but you were being annoying", which is an invitation to a new Drama. "I'm sorry you feel like that" is another kind of fake apology, often used by politicians.

If you ended up Rescuing, give the other person some respect. "Sorry, I thought you were in some kind of difficulty there. But now I see that you were doing fine."

If you ended up as a Victim, make sure that you protect yourself next time you have any dealings with that person. You might be able to get some kind of restitution. Caroline had her ex walk into her property and remove an item he claimed was 'his', though this was long after the divorce settlement. She called him and, in a polite, grown-up tone, asked for it back. He had a go at her. She quietly said that she did not want to hear this and put the phone down. Later, she called the police and simply told them the facts of the case. After some Drama – from which she stayed totally detached – including the ex refusing to talk to the police and ending up spending a night in the cells, the object was returned. However, such action is usually not possible. Learn the lesson and move on.

Forgive

Forgive yourself for getting into the Game. It sounds easy, but it can be hard, as what drew you into the Game was old stuff which won't just walk away if you ask it nicely. But remind yourself that everybody does this sort of thing from time to time.

Try and forgive the other person, too. This can be harder; a lot harder if the game has been Second or Third Degree. It can be even harder still if the person is still going round sending out exactly the same Game Invitations and getting away with it.

It always helps to remember that much, maybe all, Game playing comes from places of pain and personal / social inadequacy. Nothing in Chapter Ten, where we looked at the deep causes of Drama, was very impressive.

Forgiveness isn't an instant thing. People often say there was a moment when they really forgave x for y – but this is usually after a lot of inner work. Forgiveness happens in steps. Various writers have produced different sets. Among self-help authors, Wayne Dyer lists 15 and Deepak Chopra 7. The excellent Greater Good Science Center at Berkeley and Dr Fred Luskin of the Stanford Forgiveness Program both suggest 9.

Most writers on the subject seem to agree on certain common steps on the journey to forgiveness:

- Understand the situation as deeply as possible (this book should help)

- Don't feel you have to be reconciled to the person. You don't. If you have to deal with them, you do need to be polite, but nothing more is necessary.

- Forgiveness isn't about condoning the action.

- Forgiveness is essentially for you. It's about putting down a useless old burden.

- Move on, living a positive life. As the old motto has it, 'the best revenge is a happy life'.

Get Good Things from the Encounter

Every cloud, they say, has a silver lining. The discomfort of past mistakes can be a powerful *motivation* for future personal development. They can make you more eager to build your understanding and your resilience.

Learn *lessons*. What hooked you into the Drama? What signs were there that, in the build-up, the situation was moving up the Drama DEFCON levels? How will you spot them better next time? What will you do differently?

Get over it

Get away

Don't escalate
>You've not been 'chicken', you've been sensible
>You'll never get the last word

Ground yourself again in practical, adult activity

Discuss the episode with a sympathetic person

Reset the balance if possible:
>Apologize if you ended up as Persecutor
>Give respect if you ended up as Rescuer
>Gently reassert equality if you ended up as Victim

Forgive
>Yourself
>The other person (you don't have to reconcile)
>Allow this process to happen in steps

Motivate yourself to grow

Learn
>Use the experience as a spur to start building a better life

Chapter Thirteen

Stepping out of Sagas

In this chapter, I want to look at what to do if you are in the middle of a Saga, a long-running series of Games, with seemingly endless Switches around the Triangle, like Chris and Emma in Story One.

You are not alone. Many people in relationships are, sadly, running Sagas, as are people in workplaces or institutions of various kinds. Therapists are more often consulted about Sagas than about one-off moments of 'sucker' weakness.

Here is a seven-step process for getting out of Sagas.

First, stand back and <u>become aware</u> of what has been going on, in terms of the Drama Triangle. Who has been playing which of the roles? What are the switches? What makes them happen?

Then <u>recentre</u>. Remind yourself that you are in charge of how you see the world and how you react to it.

Third, <u>decide</u>. 'No More Games'. Draw a thick line, of whatever colour you choose, between the past and the future.

There are things that the other person does, that you know are Game Invitations but which you sometimes buy into. Now, you are not going to buy in again. You are going to react differently.

You undoubtedly send out Game Invitations, too. Now you are going to catch yourself before you do this and do something else instead. (Spotting these is usually harder than spotting the invitations that the other person sends out. To spot your own just-about-to-invite-ness, look for a sense of slightly illicit excitement, a childish sense of 'getting one over' on the other person.)

Make copies of the boxes on the next pages and use them.

The other person in this Drama sends out Game Invitations when (s)he...

1)

2)

3)

4)

Next time (s)he does this, I shall…

1)

2)

3)

4)

I send out Game Invitations to her/him when I...

1)

2)

3)

4)

In future, instead of these, I shall…

1)

2)

3)

4)

Oddly, the simple act of making a decision can change things. Years ago, a friend had a tennis coach who was a bit free with his hands (this was long before #MeToo). She decided 'enough was enough' and that she would confront his behaviour at the next session.

The next session came. She turned up on the court full of resolve – and the coach behaved respectfully then and from then on. She never said a word to him, but somehow, her body language (or something; she has no idea what) telegraphed her new intention, and that was enough.

Fourth, <u>Act</u>. Most people won't respond in this apparently telepathic way. Become an expert on spotting potential Drama and nipping it in the bud, using the tactics described in Chapter Eleven.

Fifth, <u>Stay Resolute</u>. Usually, the initial response of the Game initiator will be to ignore your new responses, to try some new Invitations or to escalate the old ones. Be alert for these. If one of them ropes you in, be gentle with yourself. This is a long-term campaign, not a one-off battle.

Jane's boss used to make patronizing and belittling comments about her. She tried ways of dealing with that, but finally decided that enough was enough, and asked for a face to face conversation with him.

In this conversation, he denied that he was being patronizing. He then accused her of not having a sense of humour and of being overcritical (switching himself to the Victim of this excess criticism and casting her as Persecutor). She politely agreed to differ. The conversation ended.

After this, a new line of negative comments began – now about Jane's starchiness. After a while, she complained about this, and the manager repeated that the fault was hers: she lacked the resilience needed for the job. If she disliked the atmosphere in the office, he said, there were plenty of people willing to take her place.

She did not give up. She didn't stew in her own sense of injustice, but let in the fresh air of third party involvement by finding a few chosen individuals to discuss the matter with. In these discussions, she described what had happened, and asked if she was being oversensitive. If the individuals had said 'yes', or even 'well, a bit', she would have changed her strategy – but they thought his reactions were out of order, too.

She began making a record of every time he behaved in an unacceptable manner. Once she had a list that she reckoned would get her taken seriously, she made a formal, undramatic complaint to the HR department – making the third party involvement more serious. She reported the facts of the various incidents – no Drama or emotion. When the head of HR asked her what she wanted to be done, Jane simply replied, 'follow whatever procedures are correct'.

A meeting with her boss was organised and overseen by the HR head, at which it was made clear that the boss was expected to take Jane's comments seriously. He tried to deflect them with humour, but the HR Head insisted he take the points on board.

At the end of the meeting, Jane did not crow or act triumphally towards the manager (Persecuting) or get all pally with him ('We'll all be good friends now')(Rescuing). Just stayed polite.

A few days later, she was putting some papers away after a long day. She saw him striding up to her desk and suddenly felt afraid – there was something in his demeanour that telegraphed aggression. But at the last moment, he seemed to change. He gave a weak smile, made some bland comment about excessive amounts of paper, and walked off again.

He moved to another department shortly afterwards.

If the resolve to resist is strong enough, Game initiators usually take the hint in the end.

Take time to <u>understand your part in the Drama.</u> Don't just blame the other person. In the story above, Jane also had a conversation on the phone to her long-time best friend Anna about these issues. Anna sympathized, but suggested that she, Jane, look at her own behaviour, too. Was there anything she was doing that encouraged this guy? Jane got angry and accused her friend of disloyalty. "Who's side are you on?" she said angrily and slammed the phone down.

Next morning, she rang Anna and apologized. She also promised to look at her own actions.

She and Anna met a few evenings later, and they had a long conversation over a bottle of wine, where Jane admitted that she didn't respect her boss, whom she thought was rude and — if she was really honest, 'common'. She admitted that she enjoyed moments where he said things that betrayed his lack of sophistication and *savoir faire*. Part of this pleasure lay in Persecutor superiority, part in Victim resentment that he was in a senior position to her.

'I never did or said anything, though,' Jane said.

Anna, a perceptive woman who understood how people can send signals subconsciously, raised her eyes to the ceiling. Jane blushed and laughed.

Jane resolved to clear this stuff from her head. The boss was a fellow human being, with faults — everybody has faults. And he was due respect because of his position within the company. She genuinely put this resolve into practice, but the damage had been done, and the unpleasantness outlined above followed.

There is an old expression: 'It takes two to tango'. In the modern world, where 'righteous' Persecutors are quick to hand out blame, the wisdom of this expression is often overlooked. But if you genuinely seek to live a better life, rather than just to impress fellow virtue-signallers, then it is always worth considering those words, and your role in any Game playing.

The world's religions advise us to leave judging others to God, and to improve ourselves instead. Classic texts from the Christian tradition include St Matthew chapter 7, verses 1 to 5 to mind ('Judge not, that ye be not judged') and the parable of the woman caught in adultery in the Gospel according to St John ('Let he who is without sin, cast the first stone'). Many humanist philosophers have made similar points.

A seventh stage is: <u>Change!</u> Go deeper into your own character. Challenge yourself. Look at Chapter Ten again – what are the big issues there that stand out for you? Which sections made you wince as you read them? Work on these issues. Talk with friends, but consider enlisting the help of a therapist or counsellor.

A Happy Ending
Chris and Emma, from Story One, didn't split up after all. They went to see a counsellor – an enlightened third party – who got them talking openly about their feelings in a grown-up way.

Chris finally admitted that when Emma said, "Let's sit down and talk", he felt scared. His instant thought was that a load of criticism was heading his way – he had already cast her as a Persecutor and himself as a Victim. He admitted he didn't like being criticized (adding, "Does anybody?"). He admitted to being insecure underneath it all.

The counsellor pointed out how Emma could have leapt onto the Triangle at this point. She got Emma to act out each of the roles:

- Rescuing: "I'm sorry, darling, I didn't realize, come and have a hug".

- Persecuting: "Huh! That's what every creep and bully says."

- A Victim competition. "You think you're insecure! You don't know what insecurity is like. When I was seventeen, I had this boyfriend who…"

Then she got Emma to simply listen with the intention of understanding his side of the story and feeling the emotions he felt as he told it: a compassionate approach.

Emma admitted that she had really wanted to hurt Chris when she made that comment about the bikes. "I can be a bitch sometimes. I don't like that side of myself, but it's there."

The counsellor then got Chris to act out Triangle role responses to this:

- Rescuing. "I think you're basically a nice person underneath it all."

- Persecuting back: "Too bloody right that side is there. And I don't think you dislike it at all. You bloody love it. It's weird…"

- Victim. "Do you know how unpleasant it is being on the end of that?"

Then she made him take a fourth, compassionate, listening approach.

They have made a commitment to talk more about feelings and to flag up whenever one of them feels themselves to be on the Triangle (or about to topple onto it). They now both feel much happier as a couple, and also reckon they have become 'better people' as the result of the therapy.

Not all Sagas have that option, however. How could Jane and her manager have been open with each other in this way?

They couldn't. But they could from then on have been polite, respectful and avoided Games. Maybe some kind of coaching would have been available within their organisation. The Persecuting manager chose not to go down that route. That was his decision. He is now bullying someone else, trapped in another Saga by his own past and by his present refusal to look at himself objectively.

Stepping out of Sagas

Sagas are very common where people are 'locked together'

A 'Seven Step Process'

    <u>1. Become aware</u> of what's going on

    <u>2. Recentre</u>

    <u>3. Decide: 'No More Games'</u>
        You will respond differently when hot buttons are pressed
        You will not send out Game Invitations

    <u>4. Act</u>

    <u>5. Stay resolute</u>
        Game players will try and undermine your decision

    <u>6. Understand your own part in the Drama</u>
        'It takes two to tango'

    <u>7. Change!</u>
        Find a therapist if necessary

The Power of Compassion

Chapter Fourteen

Stop Playing the Triangle Roles

In this chapter, I shall look at how you can challenge your tendency to play the specific Drama Triangle roles.

Remember that we probably have a 'favourite' role, but we also will play all the roles at some time, especially if we are stuck in a Saga where there are plenty of Switches. So, while one of the three categories will probably be most relevant, the others have messages, too. Ditch the Drama, role by role.

How to stop Persecuting

Loosen up. Question your own beliefs and values – are you sure you are right about everything?

Think beyond the Persecutor world-view of life as a 'zero-sum game' where for every winner there has to be a loser. Actually, most great things are achieved via co-operation.

Consider how society is held together by mutual respect, by the following of rules – especially the Golden Rule: 'Do unto others as you would have done unto you.' Think how recent events have shown the shallowness of the 'all against all' world-view.

Expand your awareness. In social situations, be curious about what other people are thinking or feeling.

Face up to those *emotions* that drive persecution.

Question your <u>anger</u>.

Karl says he has 'a right to be angry'. Ask him how or why, and he switches to Victim and starts telling you about his tough childhood.

Jez, computer-based warrior for virtue, also feels justified in his anger. Isn't 'righteous anger' – for public good – a virtue? In some situations, no doubt. But Persecution is Persecution, and has the same consequences whether it is carried out in the name of virtue or in pursuit of selfish ends. Jez may be in some ways a 'better' person than Karl, but once he gets on the Triangle, he is just another Persecutor.

A *therapist's consulting room* is a good place to work out anger issues. You can vent feelings in an environment of confidentiality: the emotion can be expressed, 'held' and then moved on from.

Social media are a poor place to express your own anger. Comments made in haste are permanently on view to people who have no idea of your better side.

The worst place to work out anger, of course, is *at home*.

Anger is part of grieving, and some Persecutors are still full of anger from uncompleted grieving processes – especially if they grew up being told that the best cure for loss was not to show any feeling.

Question your <u>aggression</u>, too. The distinction between 'assertive' and 'aggressive' can be of great help. The former is positive, ensuring you get what you need. The latter is unsocial and the stuff of Games.

All our example Persecutors in Chapter Two had some <u>sense of superiority</u>. Rather than question their own superiority to others, they would be better off questioning the whole concept. What does it mean to say that one person is superior to another? It's largely context-dependent. I am superior in my writing skills to most people. When I take my car to the garage, the mechanics are superior to me in their car-servicing skills.

Chantal clearly thinks that physical beauty is above such relativism. Such a belief is hard to change – but maybe life will teach her. It will as she gets old. These kinds of snobberies are often based on insecurity.

Finally, question your <u>fear</u>. As I've said, people who play Persecutor a lot are often lugging a great deal of fear around with them. Questioning some of the assumptions about the world above (zero-sum game etc.) can reduce this fear. Is the world really that scary?

Stop Persecuting

Loosen up

Abandon the idea of life as a 'zero-sum game'

Consider the Golden Rule
      'Do unto others as you would have them do unto you'

Be curious about other people

Question your Persecutor emotions
      Anger – a therapist can help
      Aggression
      Superiority – question the whole idea
      Fear

How to stop playing Victim

As above, ditch the 'zero-sum' view of the world. Consider it as an abundant place instead. You may well then wonder why life hasn't been that abundant to you. But maybe it has, more than you think: practice gratitude (more about that in Chapter Seventeen).

Think of society as something waiting for your contribution. If you can't think what that is right now, live with that uncertainty but don't lose faith.

Give up the Victim pay-offs. This is not easy. On modern society, victimhood carries a moral status now that it didn't a generation ago. Am I really advising you to give that up?

Yes.

What, even that brilliant chance to switch to Persecutor and do so with complete moral impunity?

Especially that. Sorry.

Face up to Victim 'favourite bad feelings'.

Passivity and helplessness are best challenged by action. Do something! Go for a walk – get your body moving. Make a list of things you need to do but have put off, and then work through it. Put a couple of relatively easy ones at the top, then a real tough one. Let yourself enjoy taking on the challenges these present. When you've done your list, treat yourself to something special.

Sadness is not a Victim emotion, but a natural response to the inevitable losses that life brings (along with all the good stuff).

However, getting stuck in sadness is a Victim experience. The natural process of grieving will involve sadness, but it will eventually fade (though never quite vanish: why should it?)

If you are stuck with sadness you seem unable to shake off, a therapist is probably the best person to talk to.

Self-pity is a Victim favourite. How do you get out of that? Action and talking stuff through can help, but I feel that self-discipline is in order here. Plus, perhaps, a bit of humour. Of all the negative emotions discussed in this book, self-pity is perhaps the most ridiculous. It's fashionable – and, I believe, right – to treat emotional experience with reverence. Most of the time. But sometimes an old-fashioned "Don't you realize how silly you look?" can be the best medicine for self-pity.

Joan says: "Sometimes I suddenly become aware that I'm moaning too much about things, and I give myself a bit of a talking to. I tell myself to smile, too. I know that sounds touchy-feely and I'm not like that, but it does seem to work."

Listen to songs like Elkie Brooks' *Fool if you Think it's Over* or (for rockers) *C'mon* by Man.

Fear can be a powerful, and often hidden, driver of Victim emotions. Read Susan Jeffers' *Feel the Fear and Do it Anyway* and follow the advice in this classic book.

Victims also need to deal with their anger. Victims, especially ones who want to be seen as nice people, hide their anger. It seeps out, of course, through 'passive aggressive' acts – the nasty dig, the anonymous note, the sulk, the nine-tenths finished piece of work.

This is probably another one for discussion with a therapist. You need to own your anger in a more honest way, then you can deal with it in a conscious, effective fashion.

Stop playing Victim

Question the zero-sum game

Consider: you have things to offer!

Forgo the Victim payoffs

Challenge your Victim emotions
     Helplessness, fear – do something!
     Stuck sadness – a therapist can help
     Self-pity – snap out of it!
     Fear – 'feel it and do it anyway'
     Hidden anger and 'passive aggression' – own the anger

How to stop Rescuing

In a way, this is the most difficult one, because there often aren't any obvious 'wrong' behaviours to fix. What's wrong in helping others?

Nothing, of course. But remember that Rescuing is about 'helping' in ways that turn out not to be very helpful. Don't stop being a nice, helpful person. Do stop making people dependent on you.

Do think before you rush in to rescue. Do they really need you or is there someone equally available but better qualified and more able to help? Do you have some kind of plan – including an exit plan?

Take deep pleasure in the sight of someone you have helped doing their own thing, without your help any longer. Good teachers do this, feeling quiet pride at the achievements of their pupils.

Allow yourself to accept help from others if you are in need.

Question the Rescuer narratives in your head. To be a good person, you don't have to ride in on your white horse and save the day, or have all the 'right' views on everything.

Allow yourself to grieve when you suffer loss, or simply to feel sad sometimes. You don't have to be jolly all the time. It's nice when you are jolly, but it's not a requirement.

Before offering help, consider exactly how you are going to do so. If you don't have the resources (including time and energy), don't make the offer.

Steer clear of obvious Victims. The first time you do this, you will probably feel ashamed of your callousness, but over time it gets easier.

Once you have clearer boundaries, you can choose to help others when you feel like it and to an extent that you know you can manage.

Adrian hated it when beggars got onto the tube and hassled passengers. He felt he was a callous bastard if he ignored them, but a sucker if he gave them any money.

He now reminds himself that the beggar has made a choice to get on the tube in the first place, and that he, Adrian, has a choice to help or not. If he's feeling generous that day, why not? If he's got other things on his mind, then he has a perfect right to ignore the beggar.

He makes a regular donation to a homeless charity.

If you feel the need to ooze virtue at all times, remind yourself that you don't have to. Question that voice that insists you be a paragon of rightness all the time (and that if you don't, you're very bad).

Stop Rescuing

Don't...
  make others dependent on you
  rush in
  offer help if you can't deliver it

Enjoy others' success

Accept...
  help if you need it
  feeling sad sometimes

Steer clear of Victims (for a while)
  Later you can help in a measured way if you choose to

Chapter Fifteen

Drama-proof yourself

Here are some more general ways you can build up your inner resistance to Drama.

Cultivate your Adult

We all think we know what 'being an adult' actually is, but it's an interesting exercise to ask – in detail – what we actually mean by that. Ask various people, and you'll get intriguingly different answers.

Joelle, who's eighteen, gives a grin and says, "Nobody can tell me what to do any longer!"

For Eric Berne, the person in their 'Adult ego-state':

- Uses logic and reason
- Thinks in terms of probabilities rather than absolutes
- seeks out factual information
- finds solutions for problems

I've always felt that Berne's was a rather narrow list. Here's a list I drew up, not from any research but just asking myself what I thought and noting the answers. Adults:

- handle criticism and setbacks
- apologize when they screw up
- keep their word

- make choices and act on them

- take responsibility for their actions

- take responsibility for others when they need to

- run their own lives

- have a measure of control over the expression of their emotions

- respect the basic rights and 'space' of other people – i.e. they have a sense of fairness

- contribute to the groups they belong to

If this sounds a bit worthy, it isn't an exhaustive list of desirable human qualities. An ideal person would also be playful, fun, affectionate, loving, imaginative, compassionate, capable of spontaneity (and no doubt other things). This list is about specifically 'adult' stuff, the safe, solid place we need to inhabit when faced by Game Invitations or our own desire to sneak onto the Triangle.

It's just one list, of course. What qualities do *you* think makes an 'adult'?

For me, an Adult…

1

2

3

4

5

6

7

8

9

10

Take your time over your list. Feel free to come back to it and tinker with it. You can add extra qualities or have fewer if you like. I've only suggested 10 because it's a nice round number.

Avoid Dramatic Thinking

Drama is encouraged by dramatic thinking. There are three main ways we do this: overgeneralizing, catastrophizing and personalization.

Overgeneralizing can involve using words like *always* ("I always screw up") or *never* ("I'll never sort this out"). It can involve making generalizations about people ("That sort of person does x..."). "All politicians are crooks," says George over his beer in The Duke's Head, casting himself as a Victim of their criminality.

By stuffing vast chunks of that incredibly complex thing called reality into tiny simplistic boxes, overgeneralizing hobbles our capacity for learning and understanding. Some politicians probably are crooks. Many have probably bent the rules at some time. But all? This kind of thinking shrinks and encrusts our world, making it small and brittle.

Yet it can often feel comfortable. It can be a 'parent ego-state' thing: many people inherit prejudices. Overgeneralizing can give the pretence of understanding, which feels safer than ignorance. "All xs are ys" sounds knowledgeable, even if it is wrong and actually rather stupid.

Overgeneralizations are often embedded in unhelpful role schemas. They can help us work ourselves up into 'favourite bad feelings', especially anger or fear. They reinforce our identification with, and performance of, the Triangle roles.

Challenge them. "Always?" "Never?" "*All* xs?"

Catastrophizing is assuming the worst from a situation.

"I find myself imagining the worst things that could happen given any course of action," says Keith. "I have to calm myself, tell myself these things are very unlikely. Like flying. Supposing the plane crashes... But I have to fly sometimes, and I get myself worked up into a state – then the flight is over and it's all been a load of fuss about nothing."

Bad things sometimes do happen, of course. Cognitive Behavioural Therapy, the therapy of choice in the British National Health Service, invites people to consider this, and then how they would deal with the problem. Almost all non-fatal difficulties can be dealt with.

The third type of Dramatic Thinking, *Personalization,* involves overestimating your own importance in the cause of things.

"My boyfriend hadn't rung me for three days," said Anna. "I began thinking, 'What did I do to make him hate me suddenly?' I went over the last time we were together, looking for clues. Then I found out he had lost his phone."

Rescuers can easily fall into the personalization trap, thinking that it's only *their* Rescuing that keeps others from falling into various abysses.

The benefits of personalization are obvious – it makes us feel important. But it can lead to people putting a lot of totally unnecessary weight on their own shoulders in a way that doesn't benefit them or anyone else.

Moderate your Speech
Cut out the instant judgement and the exaggerated damning or praise. People who describe a mediocre play as 'utterly dreadful' are getting carried away with their own loquacity and have drifted into Persecuting. The same for sports fans who describe a below par performer as 'absolute rubbish' (next week, that player scores a wonder goal or hits a

home run). This may seem trivial, but it's all part of a mindset you are trying to ditch. Like a small crack that water can seep into and cause a lot of damage, it's an easy fix. Do it.

The same follows for everything you write. Don't rush into words. Social media encourage this – resist. Stay dignified. If it means losing the virtual company of pastimers, so be it. Move on. Change.

Cancel your Triangle Role Club Memberships

In Chapter Ten, I talked about the 'benefits' of being a member of at least one, maybe three outfits: the Victim, Persecutor and Rescuer Clubs. Amongst these were a 'Loyalty Card', on which you gained points so that one day, you could enjoy a great splurge of role-playing.

Now it's time to take your nice smart Loyalty Card and cut it up.

That won't be the end of it, however. Our subconscious is always throwing seemingly random memories into our 'stream of consciousness'. Some of these will be ones where we played one of the three roles and which used to be welcomed as extra points on our Loyalty Cards.

Post-Traumatic Stress Disorder is the ultimate version of this, with one or a few dreadful memories repeatedly and unstoppably breaking in. The girl in Story Four suffered from this for many years. First she just accepted it as something she couldn't do anything about; later she saw a series of therapists, one of whom managed to help her. Fortunately, the rest of us suffer a much gentler version.

This re-emergence won't just stop. We can't control our subconscious in this way. However, we can control our response. We can welcome certain memories and reject others. Rejection is best done politely. "Sorry, but I no longer identify with that person."

Even that won't stop them coming, but it should lessen their frequency and will certainly lessen their effect.

Club membership also means interpreting the here and now in particular ways. The young man in Story Four could have dealt with sexual rejection by feeling simple natural sadness, not the anger and self-pity that got him double points on his Persecutor and Victim Club Loyalty Cards. He could, after a bit of reflection, have seen the experience as a useful life-lesson, another step on the journey, which everyone finds bumpy, towards finding a suitable partner. But he chose to file it away as evidence for his Victim world-view. You can choose differently.

When you've cut up your old membership cards, why not join a new one: the Upbeat Club? It, too, has a Loyalty Card. You already have points on it – think back to happy times (or times that were tough but where you were making real progress). Add more by having more enjoyable experiences and by helping other people. Double points if you do both at the same time! Such advice is often dismissed as corny – but who's making that judgement?

The Drama-Ditching Wheel

Coaches often ask new clients to fill in a 'Wheel'. You, the client, mark yourself on how happy you are, out of ten, about your life as experienced in various categories. You then fill in a segmented wheel with your results. 8 out of 10 for family life? Fill in that segment 80%. Health not too good at the moment? 3 out of 10? Fill in that segment 30%. And so on. The Wheel is designed to give an overview of 'where you're at' and to suggest areas where you can put work in to make your life better.

In Chapter Ten I looked at the various big payoffs from Drama. In the Drama-Ditching Wheel, I invite you to look at the areas, based on the discussion in that chapter, where you think a weakness might lead you to do Drama. Marks out of ten — do you have issues with...

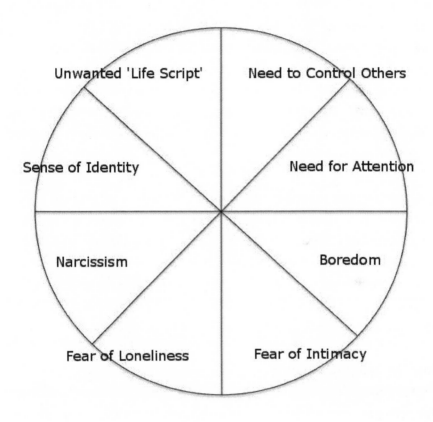

Narcissism is perhaps an odd category above: if you're really narcissistic, it's the last thing you will see yourself as. But most of us have a touch of this, and, if so, would be better people with less.

The simple act of filling the Wheel in can be thought-provoking. When it is done, of course, think carefully about your weakest areas. What can you do about them?

These are all vast topics, so a small book like this can only really set you off on whatever journeys of discovery the Wheel suggests you undertake.

Kate, tired of living out a Saga, identified her need to control others as a problem. She began by simply searching on Google, and read some of the sites that came up. Some she found bland, others unhelpful, but a number of them made really powerful points, which she noted down in a smart notebook she bought specially. One piece, that simply said 'You are allowed to have your own feelings' made her burst into tears. (Other people, of course, would look at that and think: 'Well, of course you're allowed to. Why even bother to say that?' Everyone's journey is different.) She eventually found a therapist who specialized in control issues, and worked with her.

Other therapists will specialize in other areas. A friend and fellow author, Robbie Steinhouse, uses a process to help people rewrite 'losing' Life Scripts.

And so on. There are many options.

Become More Discerning
The journey of personal development is a journey of becoming more discerning about the world around us – 'critical' not in a negative sense, but in the ability to spot cheap attempts to manipulate our susceptibility to Triangle roles.

Talk is cheap, especially on social media. More traditional media often seem no better, with low-grade newspapers running stories that are simple lures into playing Triangle roles.
Seek information from the most reliable, unbiased source you can find.

This is particularly important in the field of politics. Politicians can sow confusion with meaningless, emotive generalizations, which create the lack of clarity that Drama thrives on. They then often issue Game Invitations, demonizing (= Persecuting) opponents or social groups, casting themselves or their party as Rescuer, and casting society / the nation / 'decent people' / the environment as Victim.

Become aware of these tricks, and judge the player accordingly.

Turn on the TV and there may well be a soap opera. This will be a Game-fest, with people Switching round and round the Triangle. The same characters seem to have a boundless appetite for this. There is no resolution and no learning. Our emotions may get wound up, but to no real purpose.

By contrast, quality books, movies or theatre deal in Drama too but they don't skip the details or the consequences. We see exactly how Hamlet or Macbeth gets trapped in Drama, by their own weaknesses, and we see the mess that results. As audiences, we enjoy the ride, but we also emerge from the experience wiser and more compassionate.

This is, in a way, about becoming 'more serious'. 'Serious' doesn't mean boring. Games and acting out Triangle roles drain energy to no purpose. Lift yourself clear of that stuff, and you will have more energy for enjoying life. The truly 'serious' person values what life has to offer and makes the most of it, while at the same time being aware, compassionate, self-disciplined and thoughtful.

Drama-proof yourself

Cultivate your Adult

>A safe place to go when drama looms

Avoid Dramatic Thinking

>Overgeneralizing
>Catastrophizing
>Personalizing

Moderate your Speech

Cancel your P,V,R Club Memberships and Loyalty Cards

>'Sorry, that's not me any longer.'
>Join the Upbeat Club

The Drama-Ditching Wheel

>Become more aware of your weaknesses
>Honour *your* responses
>Do something about things you want to change

Become More Discerning

>About social and news media
>About politicians
>About culture

Chapter Sixteen

Drama-proof your World

You can take charge of your world, too. Not totally, of course, but in powerful ways that will make life a lot better.

Change the Company you Keep
If you spend much of your time pastiming or racketeering with fellow Persecutors / Victims / Rescuers – stop!

B must quit his gang. Tammy and Fran, racketeering in The Duke's Head, need to stop talking virtue and start getting involved in some projects. Jo-beth will have to leave the once-helpful Support Group that has lost its way.

Seek out positive, magnanimous, life-loving people, people you click with because you share these traits, and whose company you will enjoy. Then do stuff with them and enjoy it to the full.

Many Drama-players secretly fear that others are 'out to get them'. Consider the opposite, that life is a team game. Good relationships are active, creative things.

Navigate round the Game-Players
You're still going to have to deal with Game-players. Become better at spotting them – like that Marines sergeant major who knew the Game-players in Clive Woodward's rugby squad at once. Trust your instinct. Whose company do you find exhausting, sapping all your energy?

Don't demonize these people – that's playing Persecutor. Don't try and Rescue them, either. You're not their therapist. Simply accept that they can be difficult to deal with and plan accordingly. Brief yourself before meeting them. Remind yourself of any Game Invitations they issue and have a strategy ready for deflecting those. The best response is usually some kind of line that gives the issuer recognition but which clearly refuses to 'play ball'. "That's your view – you know I think differently, so let's agree to differ." "I understand you feel strongly about that, but we've got to do x and y today…"

Get Help on your Journey

Self-help books often recommend getting a *'growth buddy'*, someone you can talk issues through with, who helps you change and whom you help change. I was incredibly lucky to find such a person in my life when, in my thirties, I suddenly realized I couldn't carry on living my life on auto-pilot and actually had to question the assumptions I had grown up with and had been living by.

Kate joined a *discussion group* where personal development issues were debated. "We meet once a month," she says. "Everyone is really supportive. No Games get played. It's a really special space."

If you feel there is a particular area where you need to improve, *therapy* is an excellent option.

Expertise in a particular field – one you identified via the Drama-ditching wheel – is more important than the model used. And empathy is arguably the most important thing of all.

Don't get too hung up on the type of therapy (unless a model sounds repellent, in which case, obviously, avoid it). Much to the annoyance of True Believers in particular therapeutic models, research repeatedly shows that the type of therapy isn't as important as the quality of the relationship between therapist and patient.

You may have to try a few therapists to find the right one. Don't feel bad about this – you owe it to yourself to find the best person to work with. Treat money spent on 'wrong' therapists as part of your investment in your better self, not just a 'waste' (which is a Victim way of looking at things).

When you work with a therapist, be courageous. 'Hot buttons' suddenly become friends. There will be old pain behind them. "It really annoys me when…" "It really hurts when…" Now you can press them as hard as you dare and see what comes up, in the company of someone who is both compassionate and trained to deal with what emerges. Instead of hateful weak points, they can become gateways to building strength.

Help Others on their Journeys
The more you work on this material, the better you will be at helping others on theirs. Remember, this is not Rescuing. Help when asked. Celebrate others' success.

Avoid Toxic Environments
Become aware of those environments or occasions that generate stress, and avoid them where possible.

If you can't avoid them, you may be able to detoxify them a bit by setting an example of clarity, politeness and calm.

But maybe not – have the Drama DEFCON model from Chapter Eleven handy.

When you exit a toxic environment, really relish the feeling of freedom, good sense and sheer rightness that comes with that exit. One of the great tricks of toxic environments is to plant in your mind the thought that they are somehow 'normality' and that the Drama-free world is somehow inauthentic. Don't be fooled by this. Actively assert the opposite instead. Even better, do so in the company of people with a similar enjoyment of authenticity and truthfulness.

Make the World Better

This sounds rather a tall order, but we can all play our part. Small deeds of sense and kindness can ripple out to all sorts of unexpected places.

If you are a *leader*, shape the environment in which you lead by creating a culture. You do this whether you mean to or not, by your actions and attitudes, so do so consciously.

- Make clarity a key virtue. Have clear rules and rewards. Be clear at all times with others and insist they are clear with you and with each other.

- Reward any challenge to jargon and obfuscation.

- Reward Game-free behaviours such as teamwork, kindness and consideration for others.

- Make people aware of the material in this book and make it clear that Game Invitations are against the rules.

- Initially people who break the rules need to be talked to, so that they fully understand what they are doing and why it's against the culture.

- If someone isn't able to kick their Drama habit, then you have to get rid of them.

- Do all you can to minimize the Drama of such dismissals. Have a crystal-clear dismissal procedure (warnings etc.)

- Above all, remember that you lead by example.

I've mentioned *politics* and politicians in a negative context so far in this book. But politics is necessary. In a fast-changing world, public policy has to be perpetually developed to keep up with social, geopolitical and technological changes, and that is only done well if able and ethical adults get involved in drawing up and implementing such policy.

What does 'well' mean? Effective, certainly, but also one that helps sustain a good society. From the perspective of this book, a 'good' society is one that values and rewards 'adult' behaviours and attitudes, and discourages Games. One of the causes of Games is stress, and I think that the current set-up, where economic forces seem to drive ever more money into ever fewer pockets, is stress-producing. A society that creates 'winners and losers' encourages Persecutors and Victims.

This book isn't going to turn into a Communist manifesto – that idea failed disastrously. It is a call to work for a world where people aren't forced into Victim positions by poverty, or feel that they have to Persecute to avoid poverty. Somewhere in between *laissez faire* and Lenin is a society where there is both enterprise and wealth-creation *and* compassion and fairness. Quite what that society would look like is probably best discovered by practical experiment, by looking closely at facts, and by adult debate. Generalizations, 'fake news', and name-calling won't get us there. We need leaders who don't play Games and who, instead, practice adult values; leaders who tell the truth, who admit mistakes, who don't catastrophize, who don't spout meaningless generalizations, and who deeply desire the public good more than power, attention and easy admiration.

It's easy to look at the above and mutter 'dream on'. But there are actually plenty of models for this. In the UK, many backbench MPs put in long hours listening to constituents at 'surgeries'. Others work hard on legislative committees in a serious attempt to draft the best laws possible. I like to think of the amazing work that Mo Mowlam did in Northern Ireland.

If you feel inspired to become such a politician – what are you waiting for?

The rest of us will be looking on and applauding.

Drama-proof your World

Change the Company you Keep
    Positive people

Navigate round the Game-players
    Don't demonize them, just tread carefully

Get Others Involved
    A 'growth buddy'
    A personal development group
    Therapy
        Choose someone you click with, not a method
        Put your hot buttons to positive use!

Help others
    Help, not Rescue!

Avoid toxic environments
    Try and change them if you can't avoid them
    Stay strong if you can't avoid or change
    Use the Drama DEFCON model
    Get back to sanity as quickly as possible

Make the world better
    Simply being positive and kind can have 'ripple effects'
    Drama-free leadership
    Drama-free politics

Chapter Seventeen

The Art of Living without Drama

So, you've done most or some of the above, and ditched Drama. Well done!

The task isn't over, however. People who have taken the Drama out of their lives admit that sometimes it can leave a Drama-shaped hole.

"It's not so much that I miss it, actively, like I would a friend," says Katya, "but part of me says that I'll need Drama sometime in the future, because in my past I was such an addict. I don't crave it any longer, but I fear that the craving is waiting round the corner…"

It doesn't have to be. Katya has actually learnt how to spot potential Dramas and avert them.

There can be a temptation to make a Drama of resisting the temptation to do Drama, like a reformed alcoholic agonizing when faced with an open bottle.

It doesn't have to be like that, either. The more you practice resisting Drama, the less of a Drama that resistance becomes, and the more it becomes second nature and your energy naturally begins to get spent on more useful, consciously chosen things. This is where the rewards really flow in.

'How to live a flourishing, fulfilling life' would make another book. I shall make a few observations here.

Positive Psychology

This branch of psychology has only taken off this century, though its roots go back to the 1990s, when researchers like Martin Seligman began asking what actually makes people happy.

Up till that point, there had been plenty of theorizing on the subject, but little real research. Seligman decided to start with a blank sheet of paper, and simply find out what actually did make people happy over a period of time. The research was carried out (and is still being carried out) in as many different cultures as possible.

What he found was quite startling. Some big life-changing events were not guaranteed to bring happiness – marriage, children, promotion at work, more money. Other things did bring lasting happiness. ('Doing more Drama' was not one of them!) These turned out to be largely constant across cultures and not to have changed since the research programme began.

The thing most correlated with happiness is the *quality of personal relationships*, with partner, family, friends and other circles of acquaintanceship around us. (So clearly, marriage and children can bring happiness – but only if the marriage works and the children are cherished.) This raises a question, of course: what do they mean by 'quality'?

From the perspective of this book, I propose that quality in relationships is about two things: lasting trust and intimacy (look back to Chapter Ten for a definition of the latter). One way people use Drama is to avoid real intimacy. Drama-free, you can now let yourself pursue and enjoy it to the full, accepting and being accepted by other people and enjoying their company.

Another key correlate to happiness is a sense of *gratitude*. Gratitude to other people who have helped us, but on a more general level for all the blessings of life. This broader gratitude can come easier to someone with a specific religious faith, as there is a deity to feel grateful to. But even a convinced atheist can still simply feel gratitude. Gratitude doesn't have to have an object.

Positive psychologists recommend keeping a gratitude diary, noting down each day three things you feel grateful for. They also recommend writing a letter of gratitude to someone who has helped you in the past. Ideally, they say, you should then take it to them and read it to them. I think that putting it in the post is fine – a live reading might slip into Rescuing.

They stress the value of *savouring* small pleasures. Rather than wolfing down breakfast – stop. Take it slow and really appreciate the taste. On the way to work, enjoy the view. The receptionist at your office has a nice smile: take a moment to smile back, or even compliment them on it.

Linked to this is the ability to do ordinary stuff with brightness, awareness and attention – the now fashionable (but actually very ancient) idea of *mindfulness*.

I mentioned mindfulness in Chapter Eleven, as a tool to use in the heat of the moment, when Drama is looming and you need to create some mental space for yourself. I also said that the regular mindfulness practice makes the creation of such escape-hatches easier. Now is the time to consider such regular practice.

Unless you live at the South Pole, there will be someone near you running mindfulness courses (and even there, it's only a matter of time before an enterprising penguin sets one up). The eight-session

Mindfulness-based Stress Reduction (MBSR) course developed by academic and writer Jon Kabat-Zinn is now run all round the world by licensed teachers. If you can't get on one of these, there are many apps and YouTube videos featuring guided mindfulness meditations.

You can begin, without any courses or apps, by simply concentrating on everyday acts.

Take brushing your teeth. It's the sort of thing that the subconscious mind has long taken control of and is now quite happy to get you to do without any conscious thought on your part. Become conscious of it again. Notice the sound of the tap running. Notice the smell and the taste of the toothpaste. Notice the feel of the brush – the handle in your hand; the bristles when they touch your gums. What is the quality of light in the bathroom? A yellowish electric bulb? Sun streaming in through a window? And so on.

This is a bit like savouring, but when savouring, you are meant to really concentrate on what is pleasurable. Here, the exercise is more about noticing. If you find a particular piece of noticing pleasurable, maybe allow yourself a brief moment of enjoyment, then move on to noticing the next thing.

This reclaiming of learnt routines can add a new layer of meaning to life (one of the benefits that Drama was supposed to provide). In his poem *The Elixir*, written back in 1633 (human nature hasn't changed), the great English mystic George Herbert wrote:

> *Teach me, my God and King,*
> *In all things Thee to see,*
> *And what I do in anything*
> *To do it as for Thee.*

All may of Thee partake:
Nothing can be so mean,
Which with his tincture—"for Thy sake"—
Will not grow bright and clean.

A servant with this clause
Makes drudgery divine:
Who sweeps a room as for Thy laws,
Makes that and th' action fine.

This is the famous stone
That turneth all to gold;
For that which God doth touch and own
Cannot for less be told.

This poem can, I feel, be deeply enjoyed by anyone with a spiritual sense, not just adherents of a specific faith. I find it particularly intriguing because it says something about Life Scripts. George Herbert's room-sweeper, going about his or her routine work, would seem to have the ultimate banal script. But through their attentiveness and their sense of the quiet fullness of life, they prove themselves to be winners.

At the other end of the scale, experiencing moments of mind-blowing *awe* is important. Every now and then, attend to something full-on amazing, like a great piece of music, a special view or amazing sex with your partner. (Positive psychologists don't recommend drug- or alcohol-induced awe.) Then come back to earth again, enriched.

The simple practice of *kindness* also seems to boost personal happiness. This is not Rescuing – "Look everybody, what a good person I'm being!" – but doing something nice for someone else, quietly and without self-congratulation.

Positive psychologists also stress the value of having *compassion* for others. This brings us neatly back to where this book began, because the creator of the Triangle, Stephen Karpman, believes that this was the most important virtue of all.

Compassion begins with a sense that, as human beings, we are all 'in the same boat'. We are in many ways amazing, but we are also vulnerable. As we grow up, we experience traumas (to varying degrees) and encounter disappointments and doors that slam in our face. We are taught rubbish by significant others. Yet we also desire truth and wholeness...

The compassionate intellect will grasp the above, and understand the common troubled but aspirant humanity that we all share.

The compassionate heart will sense what it must be like to feel how others feel. There is a part of the brain, the 'mirror neuron' system, which appears to be hard-wired to do this, though some very damaged people seem to lack it.

I doubt that this neuron system allows us to feel new emotions, however. Compassion requires depth. If we think we've never felt blind rage, furious jealousy or animal lust, we will find compassion difficult. Such is the value of maturity, of having made mistakes.

A third aspect of compassion, perhaps, is a determination to use it as much as possible, to have it as the 'default state' when faced with a challenging individual or situation.

Armed with a compassionate, humane intellect, the capacity to feel others' pain (without getting flooded by it), and a determination to bring those qualities to bear on any situation, we can truly enter the world in a positive, open frame of mind.

Positive Psychology has been criticized as being 'Pollyanna-ish', of trying to Rescue humanity, with our inevitable flaws and the sadnesses that inevitably come our way, by slapping a perpetual grin onto our face. This criticism seems particularly relevant right now.

But the criticism is simplistic. The discipline teaches *resilience* in the face of bad stuff, not denial. It accepts that authentic sadness is part of life, but says sadness is something that has to be experienced then moved on from, not by sweeping under a metaphorical carpet but accepting as a part of a much bigger whole. The reality of a happy life is not perpetual jollity but a sense that joy is natural and proper, that it is a natural state we can, and have a right to, return to when negative events push us away from it and once we have come to terms with those events. Positive psychology teaches us how to cultivate an aware joyfulness, that doesn't force itself into every situation, but is waiting for us as we go through hard times.

A Positive Schema

In Chapters Two, three and Four, I looked at the 'schemas', the self-reinforcing aspects of the Persecutor, Victim and Rescuer mindsets. Now, develop a Positive Schema instead.

Encouraging Emotions

We can't get into a Tardis and re-run our childhood. But we can, up to a point, parent ourselves. We can reward ourselves for feeling the kinds of emotion we truly want to feel. This might sound odd, but remember how divided the subconscious can be, and how we may have been discouraged from feeling certain things as children. "Don't be cheerful," we may have been told, or "Don't be caring." Time to unlearn these lessons.

That old discouragement can often manifest itself via a kind of semi-aware running commentary on our feelings. "Feeling cheerful? Huh! That won't last!" "Don't be fooled. Caring's for suckers."

We can take control of this commentary. We can interrupt it when it gets negative. We can challenge it. "Who says it won't last?" "There's a lot more to real life than just getting stuff over on other people!" We can substitute our own positive commentary.

Discouraging Emotions (?)

I'm not sure that suppressing negative emotions is a good thing. We need to face them and admit them, after which we can make an adult choice whether to act on them – the act of admitting often takes away a lot of their power, which partially comes from being hidden. This admitting should be an inner process, or it can be done with a therapist or someone we totally trust. 'Admitting anger' by blurting it out on social media is not the way forward.

Learning Positive Behaviours

It might sound demeaning, but at least part of the way we learn is the same as how Pavlov's dogs learnt: simple 'stimulus and reward'. We can 'train ourselves' in positive behaviours.

The savouring enjoined on us by Positive Psychology is an exercise in that. Don't just enjoy the taste of that glass of wine, enjoy the enjoying. Even better, remind yourself that enjoying simple pleasures is part of something bigger, a positive, optimistic, life-embracing mindset. You're not just enjoying this wine for yourself, but you're making a statement to yourself that pleasure is good. The philosopher Spinoza said, "There cannot be an excess of joy: it is always good." He lived a quiet, Drama-free life.

We can loosen up physically, maybe even use new gestures.

Smile more: it sounds corny, but it does have a positive effect – especially as part of a systematic self-recreation.

Interpretations, Beliefs and Values

Another part of the schema is intellectual: what we believe, how we interpret things. Jacquie says, 'I used to get so angry if someone pulled in front of me in traffic. Now I'm curious why and let them get on with it."

At the heart of the Positive Schema lies a new view of the world. Not one we might have written as a worried 5-year-old, but one we choose as adults. It can take a while to change our beliefs: there'll be a lot of evidence stored in our memories to support the old, dark view, and a lot in the world 'out there'.

Evidence for a positive view of the world is all around us once we start looking for it. The terrible outbreak of corona virus has provided great examples of humanity at its best.

We can also find positive models in stories, real or fictional: Nelson Mandela or Florence Nightingale, Robin Hood or Elizabeth Bennett.

We can choose life-enhancing values: compassion, kindness, humanity.

We can come up with some positive maxims. 'Nice guys finish first.' Why not? They may not end up mega-rich or powerful, but they lead happier and more fulfilled lives, if Berne's concept of the 'winning script' is true. Find your own maxims that speak powerfully to you.

Memories
I'm not sure if the brain can be stopped from bringing up random, bad old memories, but we can certainly counter this by consciously enjoying happy memories. Don't let the photo album gather dust on a high shelf. Have a playlist of music with happy associations (or music that just makes us happy). Reminisce: older people are often lampooned for this, but it's a healthy thing to do (unless it slides into Victim-playing, via "Of course nowadays things are much worse...")

All the above elements, taken on their own, may seem rather jangling and over-optimistic. But taken together they reinforce one another, creating what systems theorists call a virtuous circle, where an improvement in one part of the system leads to improvements in other parts, which lead to improvements somewhere else (and so on). This is the opposite of the dark spiral that people in bad places can get into, the 'vicious circle', where bad things just lead to worse things. (You may have experienced vicious circles. If you have, use the painful awareness of their power, turn the experience on its head, and move towards flourishing.)

The Positive Schema is not a recipe for self-delusion. It is a consistent, structured way of looking at and living in the world. It doesn't deny the existence of difficulty, suffering or injustice, but offers ways of overcoming these things rather than just playing into their hands (playing into their hands is what Drama does). It puts them in context.

The psychologist Erik Erikson looked at various stages of life, and saw the final one as a battle between despair and a serene acceptance of life as miraculous but flawed. Winners end up holding the latter view. Drama, a loser's game, drags us towards the former, despairing one.

In the end, Drama is an illusion. Rather than living authentically, it makes us act out pretend versions of reality. We can do better. We can grow and change. We have the knowledge and we have the power to ditch Drama and to move on to better, truer things.

Living without Drama

Don't' make a Drama of not doing Drama any longer!
>Relax
>
>Believe in your capacity to ditch it…
>
>… and put your energy into better things

Positive Psychology
>Good personal relationships (intimacy)
>
>Gratitude
>
>Savouring
>
>Mindfulness / attention
>
>Awe
>
>Kindness
>
>Compassion
>
>Resilience
>
>Coming to terms with sadness
>
>Joy as a natural state

Create a 'Positive Schema' of self-reinforcing:
>Emotions
>
>Beliefs / values
>
>Memories and evidence

We don't have to live dramatically
>We can choose better

Where to Learn More

Stephen Karpman's site offers many articles: he is one of those people who keeps on coming up with new ideas and concepts. It is full-on TA, however, so it is best to familiarize yourself with the concepts before visiting it.

He has also written a book, *A Game-Free Life*. If you want to pursue the topic of the Drama Triangle further, this book is brimming with ideas. As with all his work, it is best approached armed with some knowledge of TA.

TA Today by Ian Stewart and Vann Joines is probably the best place to get this knowledge. It is a thorough, logical (albeit rather dry) setting out of TA and its models. (As I've said, some TA concepts seem to be more powerful than others. Make your own mind up about how deeply you believe the various bits of TA.)

Games People Play is Eric Berne's original work on Drama. It is aimed at the general reader. Berne's style can be irritating, and he can be inconsistent: he calls a number of behaviour patterns 'Games' that aren't (by his own definition) Games at all, but simply pastimes or racketeering. This book was in many ways superseded by the Drama Triangle, which captured its essence, tightened the logic and simplified things substantially. Still, it's a classic.

The Power of TED by David Emerald presents the Triangle – and a positive alternative to it – in the form of a narrative.

I've already mentioned *How to Break Free of the Drama Triangle and Victim*

Consciousness, by Barry and Janae Weinhold. This contains some useful self-help exercises. They argue that Drama is largely caused by people competing to be Victims.

In my last chapter, I discuss Positive Psychology as a model of Game-free living. There are numerous books on this. I like *The How of Happiness* by Sonja Lyubomirsky, but there are many others.

And finally...

Please note that this book is written to inform. It is not intended to be a substitute for professional mental health / medical diagnosis or treatment. Always seek the advice of your doctor, therapist or other qualified health provider on questions regarding a mental health or medical condition. Never disregard professional advice or delay in seeking it because of something you have read in this book.

The content of this book is the result of much study, but there may be errors or omissions in it, and I disclaim any liability for these.

I had to write the above paragraphs for legal reasons, but I mean them. The first one is particularly important. If you feel you are suffering mental health issues, go and see a therapist. Please. The best book in the world is no substitute for a one-to-one relationship with a skilled and caring professional.

I'd like to end by thanking a few people who have helped me on my (unfinished) journey towards understanding the Triangle. Obviously, Eric Berne and Stephen Karpman for their amazing work – but especially Dr Karpman, with whom I have had some enjoyable conversations. I learnt TA from Nick Irving and Robbie Steinhouse – two outstanding teachers. I'd also like to thank Sue Gee and my wife Rayna, two fellow students of psychology with whom I shared many long discussions. Also, the wonderful Diane Shepherd, with whom I practiced co-counselling, and the excellent teachers who taught the Counselling Diploma at Norwich City College, Norfolk, UK, back in the 1990s.

Please get in touch if you have any thoughts about
this book and its contents.
I'd love to hear from you.
My email is chris@chriswest.info.

And if you found it helpful and interesting,
please tell your friends and colleagues.

Thank you for your time and attention.